CAMBRIDGE INTRODUCTION TO WORLD HISTORY
GENERAL EDITOR · TREVOR CAIRNS

Julius Caesar

Graham Tingay

CAMBRIDGE UNIVERSITY PRESS
Cambridge
New York   Port Chester
Melbourne   Sydney

Published by the Press Syndicate of the University of Cambridge
The Pitt Building, Trumpington Street, Cambridge CB2 1RP
40 West 20th Street, New York, NY 10011–4211, USA
10 Stamford Road, Oakleigh, Melbourne 3166, Australia

First published 1991

Printed in Great Britain by the University Press, Cambridge

British Library cataloguing-in-publication data
Tingay, Graham, 1926–
    Julius Caesar.
    1. Ancient Rome. Caesar, Julius 100 B.C. – 44 B.C. –
    Biographies.
    I. Title.
    937.05092

Library of Congress cataloging-in-publication data
Tingay, Graham.
    Julius Caesar / Graham Tingay.
        p.   cm. – (Cambridge introduction to world history)
    ISBN 0-521-36738-7
    1. Caesar, Julius. 2. Rome – History – Republic, 265–30 B.C.
    3. Heads of state – Rome – Biography. 4. Generals – Rome –
    Biography.
    I. Title.   II. Series.
    DG261.T55   1990
    937′.05092 – dc20   90-1845 CIP
    [B]
ISBN 0 521 36738 7

DS

Front cover: *The Ides of March (see page 4).*

Back cover: *The frieze comes from the Ara Pacis Augustae (the Altar of Augustan Peace). It portrays members of Augustus' family, priests and representative Roman citizens. Their calm and dignified appearance is intended to emphasise the prosperity and peace of Augustus' reign in contrast to the troubled years of Julius Caesar's time.*

Title page: *This denarius was struck in 44 B.C.; the inscription reads CAESAR: DICT PERPETUO – 'Caesar, Dictator for Life', and shows him wearing the laurel wreath.*

Note on the glossary: The words printed in *italic* in the text appear in the Glossary on page 48.

Acknowledgements
The author and publisher would like to thank the following for permission to reproduce illustrations:

Front cover The Bridgeman Art Library Ltd; back cover The Ancient Art & Architecture Collection; title page, pp. 5, 11, 38, 46 Courtesy of the Trustees of the British Museum; pp. 8, 10, 15, 18, 22, 24 Archivi Alinari; pp. 14 (top), 16 The Mansell Collection; pp. 14 (bottom), 43 Deutsches Archäologisches Institut, Rome; p. 20 © Macdonald Educational Limited, 1975. Reproduced by permission of Simon & Schuster Young Books, Hemel Hempstead, UK; p. 32 From *Brittany* by P.R. Giot, published by Thames & Hudson, London; p. 42 Reproduced by permission of the Syndics of the Fitzwilliam Museum; p. 47 Musei Vaticani.

Maps by Jeff Edwards.

Other illustrations on pp. 11, 13, 34, 36 by Hemesh Alles.

Contents

The Ides of March   page 4
Sources   4
    Written evidence   4
    Archaeological evidence   5

1 The making of the man, 100–70 BC   6
    Family, education and marriage, 100–81 BC   7
    Optimates versus populares   10
    Marius and the new army   10
    Civil war in Italy   11
    Sulla as Dictator   12
    Caesar seeks experience   12
    The army, the lawcourts, the pirates   12
    First steps in office: Caesar becomes military
        tribune   13
    Caesar becomes quaestor and senator   14

2 The rise to power, 69–60 BC   15
    Caesar in Spain, 69 BC   15
    Caesar's election campaign: money problems   16
    Growing popularity   17
    Caesar becomes High Priest and praetor 17
    Catiline's conspiracy   17
    The Clodius affair   19
    Governor in Spain, 61 BC – victories and riches   19
    The loss of a triumph   20
    Caesar makes a pact with Pompey and
        Crassus, 60 BC   21

3 The consulship, 59 BC   22
    Caesar's proposal for an agrarian law   22
    Failure in the senate   22
    Success with the people   23
    Bibulus versus Caesar   23
    New laws and proposals   24
    The triumvirate under strain   26

4 The Gallic War, 58–50 BC   27
    Caesar defeats the Helvetii, 58 BC   27
    Caesar overruns northern Gaul, 57 BC   29
    Winter 57–56 BC: politics in Rome   30
    56 BC: revolt on the north-west coast   30
    55 BC: Caesar exterminates two whole tribes,
        then crosses the Rhine and the Channel   31
    54 BC: the second invasion of Britain and
        revolt in Gaul   32
    53 BC: Caesar's vengeance   33
    52 BC: the great rebellion   33
    51–50 BC: the pacification of Gaul   35

5 The Civil War, 50–45 BC   37
    The end of the triumvirate   37
    Caesar under threat   37
    Caesar versus Pompey   37
    Caesar is declared a public enemy   38
    Crossing the Rubicon   38
    The widespread war   39
    Caesar in Spain, 49 BC   39
    Caesar faces Pompey in Greece, 48 BC   41
    The battle of Pharsalus   41
    Egypt and Asia Minor, 48–47 BC   41
    Africa, 46 BC   42
    Triumph in Rome   42
    The last campaign: Spain, 46–45 BC   42

6 Towards the New Rome   43
    Reform and reconstruction   43
    Honours for Caesar   44
    Caesar as king?   44
    Supreme power   45
    The future of the republic   45
    Conspiracy   46
    After Caesar   47

Glossary   48

THE IDES OF MARCH

Soon after 10 o'clock in the morning of 15 March 44 BC – the day the Romans called the Ides of March – Julius Caesar walked through the streets of Rome to the Assembly Rooms in Pompey's theatre, where he had summoned a meeting of the senate, Rome's governing body. As Caesar went in, the senators rose in his honour. Marcus Brutus and his friends took their places behind his chair.

Tillius Cimber came up to Caesar, begging that his brother might be allowed to return from exile. A group of senators gathered round as if to support Cimber's request. Caesar sat down, waving Cimber away. Then Cimber tugged Caesar's toga down as if to make sure that he was paying attention, and this imprisoned Caesar's hands and prevented him from rising. Casca, standing behind Caesar, struck him in the neck with a dagger. Caesar turned and grasped the dagger, crying, 'Casca, you villain, what are you doing?' Then the whole group produced daggers and struck, again and again. As he sank to the ground, Caesar covered his head with his toga. Drenched with blood from some twenty-three wounds, he fell at the feet of the statue of Pompey, once Caesar's great rival, who had himself been stabbed to death four years earlier.

As most of the senators gazed in horror, Brutus spoke out to explain what had been done; but the senators rushed out, spreading terror and confusion among the people. The conspirators were left looking at each other in dismay.

The murder had been planned by some sixty of Rome's most influential citizens, led by Marcus Brutus and Cassius. Many of them had been Caesar's closest friends. They had killed the greatest Roman of his time, arguably one of the greatest men known to history. In Shakespeare's *Julius Caesar*, one of his bitterest enemies, Cassius, says of him: 'He doth bestride the narrow world like a Colossus, and we petty men walk under his huge legs and peep about to find ourselves dishonourable graves.' The sheer drama of what happened on that day has gripped people's imaginations ever since. The front cover picture is from a painting in which the artist, Vincenzo Camuccini (1773–1844), seems to have imagined the scene as the tragic climax of a grand opera. If the death of Caesar is the most famous assassination in history, what was it about him that made it so?

Sources

This book is about a man who died over 2,000 years ago. How do we know so much about him? There are two main kinds of evidence, dating from Roman times, on which this book is based.

public libraries. When these copies wore out, new copies were sometimes made in later centuries, usually on parchment. The revival of interest in classical writers during the Renaissance (in the fifteenth and sixteenth centuries AD) led scholars to search out all the Latin and Greek texts they could find. Printed editions of nearly all surviving works of Latin and Greek literature had been produced by the end of the fifteenth century AD, and they have been reprinted ever since.

1 Written evidence

The Romans wrote and published books. Copies were handwritten in ink on papyrus, which is much like paper though made in a very different way, and kept in private homes and

Works written in Caesar's lifetime

- Caesar himself published two books covering the last fourteen years of his life: *Commentarii de bello Gallico* and *Commentarii de bello civili*. (The last and eighth book of the Gallic War, and the continuation of the Civil War, known as the *Bellum Alexandrinum*, were written by Aulus Hirtius, one of Caesar's officers and friends.)

- Cicero, a contemporary statesman, made a great number of speeches about Roman affairs of the time, and many of these were published. Soon after his death, Cicero's secretary published a collection of nearly a thousand letters exchanged between Cicero and other statesmen, and these give us a vivid insight into 'behind-the-scenes' political activities.
- Sallust, who died in 35 BC, published a history of the Catilinarian conspiracy (p. 17–19).

All these have survived, but only a few fragments of any other contemporary evidence have come down to us.

Historical writing from the Roman Empire

Of other surviving histories, historical summaries or commentaries written after Caesar's death, the most important for us were composed by:

- Plutarch (AD 46–120), who wrote, in Greek, biographies of Mark Antony, Caesar, Cato, Cicero, Crassus, Lucullus, Marius, Pompey, and Sertorius, amongst others;
- Suetonius (AD 70–160), who wrote the Lives of the first twelve emperors, beginning with Julius Caesar;
- Appian (fl c. AD 160): the part of his 'Civil Wars' covering the period from Marius and Sulla to 34 BC survives;
- Dio Cassius (AD 150–235), wrote a 'Roman History' in 80 books, 24 of which, covering the years 68 BC to AD 54, survive.

There are in addition hundreds of other books written about Julius Caesar over the last few centuries. These are based on the same evidence from Roman times, but the opinions of the authors about the facts which they have gathered can be very different.

2 Archaeological evidence

The most obvious examples are the building works ordered by Caesar, such as the Basilica Julia, whose foundations can still be seen in Rome in the Roman Forum, or the siege works built by Caesar or his enemies in Gaul, for example at Alesia.

A number of inscriptions, that is written records in stone, such as laws, dedications of buildings, tombstones etc., survive from this period. They are not nearly so frequent or so helpful for our subject, though, as later inscriptions are for the times of the emperors.

However, many hundreds of coins have come down to us from the first century BC. Until about 120 BC, bronze and silver coins issued by the senate showed the head of Roma on one side (the reverse), and perhaps some god in a chariot on the other (the obverse). But from c.120 BC, the obverse often showed some political or historical achievement by some prominent citizen. From c.100 BC, these 'historical' scenes became much more frequent, and often had political overtones – as a sort of propaganda. Then great generals like Sulla and Pompey, when issuing coins on their campaigns, did not hesitate to illustrate their own successes on their coins. Julius Caesar cheerfully followed their example, and the coins he issued as Dictator were the first to show the portrait of a living Roman. You will see from examples in this book how such coins help to illuminate history for us.

This coin, issued c. 95 BC, shows how the citizens voted. They walked along a narrow raised gangway, took a ballot from an official (the central figure) and dropped it into the appropriate urn set at the end.

1 The making of the man, 100–70 BC

On the 13th day of the month Quinctilis, mid-summer 100 BC, in a busy quarter near the centre of Rome, a baby boy was born to Aurelia, the wife of Gaius Caesar. Some fifty-five years later, the month Quinctilis was renamed Julius in his honour. The baby's full name, like his father's, was Gaius Julius Caesar.

Though his family was aristocratic, it was neither very wealthy nor very well known. But his father's sister, his aunt Julia, was married to Gaius Marius, the most brilliant general and most important statesman in Rome. As Caesar grew up, he must have regarded his uncle Marius as a sort of super-human figure. So it is hardly surprising that Caesar dreamed of the same sort of success for himself. 'Success', to a boy from such a family, could mean only one thing, a career in politics and government, and, if lucky, the consulship of Rome.

The first *consuls* of Rome had been appointed in 509 BC. When the city was founded, according to tradition in 753 BC, it was just one of dozens of small independent cities in Italy. A line of kings ruled it, but their government had become so harsh that the people threw out the seventh king, and the name of 'king' was always hated by the Romans after that. Their place was taken by two consuls elected by the people each year. The consuls were chosen from the *senate*, the city council which had once advised the kings, and now, with 300 members, had become the main governing body of the state. At first only *patricians* could become consuls. The patricians were the aristocrats of Rome, and were only a small propor-tion of the total body of citizens. The rest of the citizens were known as the *plebs*, or *plebeians*. But later the consulship, and every other official post too, was open to any citizen.

By about 270 BC Rome had taken control of all Italy south of the river Rubicon. Next came a long struggle with Carth-age, the great naval and merchant power in north Africa. The Romans defeated the Carthaginians and were able to take Sicily, Sardinia, Corsica and parts of Spain and north Africa from them. Encouraged by her new strength, Rome sent her armies further overseas, and so acquired an empire embracing most of the countries round the Mediterranean. The Romans called these countries *provinces*.

Industry and trade flourished, and wealth poured into Rome. By 100 BC nearly a million people lived in it, the rich in great houses, but most in crowded blocks of apartments, noisy, smelly, and lacking any sanitation. At the centre of the city was the Forum, the main square, surrounded by rather unimpressive public buildings. Near the Forum lay the Subura, a busy, dirty and cosmopolitan district, with rich and poor, shopkeepers and manufacturers, all packed in together. It was here that the Caesar family lived.

Roman names

Men in *patrician*, or aristocratic, families had three names, *praenomen*, *nomen* and *cognomen*, like *Gaius Julius Caesar* or *Marcus Tullius Cicero*. The *nomen* end-ing in *-ius* indicated the *gens*, or clan, to which the person belonged. The *cognomen* indicated the family branch, and this was the name by which he was normally called by his colleagues, while the personal forename, *praeno-men*, was only used by relatives or close friends. In English we usually use only one of the names, e.g. Cicero, or Livy, and sometimes we know only one or two of the three names.

The women of such families legally had no name at all, but were called by the feminine form of the gens name, e.g. Cicero's daughter was known as Tullia, and Caesar's daughter was known as Julia. Of course affec-tionate personal names were used in the family to avoid confusion.

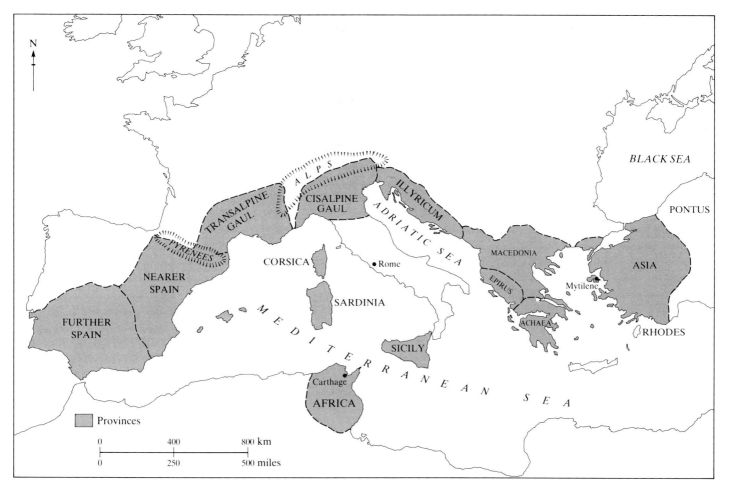

The Roman empire when Julius Caesar was born, 100 BC

Family, education and marriage, 100–81 BC

Julius Caesar's father was *praetor* (a judge, see table on p. 9) in 92 BC. In the next year he became a provincial governor: he never became consul. Though we cannot know when Julius Caesar himself began to think of his future, his family would not have wasted much time. The best start for a political career was to be born into a family with ancestors who had been consuls. Such families were called *nobiles* – a name which originally meant well-known or famous. Caesar's family was noble, though there had been no consul in it for over 150 years, and so it was not very influential. But outsiders could sometimes make their way to the top. These outsiders were called 'new men', and Marius, Caesar's uncle, was himself a 'new man'. By marrying into the Julian clan he had acquired some of its prestige, and then his success had in turn lent it some of his own fame and influence.

Caesar had therefore a promising start, and the whole purpose of his education was to ensure success for him in public life. He learnt first, of course, to read, write and do simple arithmetic, but after that most of his time was spent on

Gaius Marius 157–86 BC, Julius Caesar's uncle. Distinguished army service brought him the support of an aristocratic family, the Metelli. But when at 38 he was elected tribune of the plebs he was not afraid of proposing laws which offended the aristocrats, and looking for support from the people.

Greek and Latin literature and philosophy. And these were only a background for his study of law and of oratory (the art of speaking in public). For a young man without a great fortune, success only came from being noticed for a good performance in the lawcourts or in debates in the senate, and for this hardly anything mattered more than the ability to speak well. This skill was not learnt at a school. Tutors were hired to guide a young man's progress. He would also go as a pupil to a prominent lawyer, and listen to him discussing their cases with people who had consulted him. The lawcourts in Rome, grouped around the Forum and open to the public – they were a popular 'entertainment' – also saw a lot of the young Caesar and his friends. Here they could listen to the arguments of the prosecution and defence, and see how the skill or clumsiness of a speaker affected the jury. They could expect to continue this sort of practical education, until the age of eighteen or nineteen.

Caesar was only fifteen when, soon after the death of his father, he married Cornelia, the daughter of the consul Cinna. However, he stayed in the family home, of which he was now technically the head, and continued his education. Such early marriages were common among aristocratic families in Rome. The purpose was to link two families closely, for a purely political advantage, but within a few years Caesar's marriage was to bring his life into danger. It is impossible for us to understand this danger, or any part of Caesar's career, without some idea of what politics and government were in his time. The next few pages will make the situation clearer.

The government of Rome

Although Rome had grown from a small city to a great empire, its system of government had hardly changed. The government of the Roman empire was still the government of the city of Rome. There were no representatives from other towns in Italy, or other countries in the empire. The government was shared between the city council, its officials and the people.

The *SENATE* was the name given to the city council which took the major share of government. Originally it consisted only of *patricians*, or aristocrats, but soon it was open to any adult male citizen, in theory at least. Though its size varied, for most of Caesar's life the senate had 600 members who had gained automatic entry to it when elected junior magistrates by the people. Once selected in this way, senators served for the rest of their lives.

All government officials were called *MAGISTRATES*, and were elected by the people. They were unpaid, and held office for one year. The magistracies had to be held in strict order, and a minimum age was set for each of them:

The *PEOPLE*; The English word is confusing in that it refers to two groups of Romans:
1. The *populus*: this was the whole body of male citizens, including both patricians and plebeians. It excluded minors, women and slaves. (Politically, women remained under the control of their fathers or husbands, and had no rights at all as individuals. They could not vote or hold any political office. Of course in the family setting they must have had as much influence as they have today.) The populus was occasionally summoned, by consuls or praetors, to meet in order to
   * elect consuls, praetors, quaestors and curule aediles
   * declare war or peace
   * enact laws
   * confirm death sentences.
2. The *plebs*: the plebeians only. It was summoned by tribunes of the people (*tribuni plebis*) to
   * elect plebeian aediles, and tribuni plebis
   * vote on proposals put to it by the tribuni plebis: its

decisions made in this way were called *plebiscita*, had the force of law, and affected the whole people (populus)
- enact laws passed in the senate (in the same way as meetings of the populus.

The phrase 'people's assembly' used in this book normally refers to the assembly of the plebs.

— — — — — — — — — — — — — — — — — —

This is the *cursus honorum*, the stairway of public offices held in succession by those Romans who made their careers in government service and politics.

Censor	2 selected every five years, but served for only 18 months. Revised the senate lists. Also made contracts for public works, tax collection etc. Only ex-consuls were eligible.
Consul	2 selected each year. Summoned and presided over the senate. Could become provincial governors the following year. Commanded the armies in war. Minimum age 43.
Praetor	8 elected each year. They looked after the administration of justice in Rome and Italy. Could become provincial governors the following year. Commanded the armies in war. Minimum age 40.
Aedile	2 'curule' (patrician), 2 plebeian aediles elected each year. They looked after the city, i.e. streets, traffic, water supply, building regulations, public games, etc. Minimum age 37.
OR *Tribunus plebis*	10 tribunes, plebians only, each year. Could veto any act of senate or other magistrates. Presided over plebeian assemblies, where decisions had force of law over all the people.
	Neither office legally necessary, but in practice essential for ambitious men.
Quaestor	20 each year. 2 in charge of Treasury at Rome; others helped provincial governors in financial and military duties. Quaestors automatically became senators. Minimum age 30.

20 minor posts in the administration, e.g. in the mint, prisons, justice in Italian cities, maintenance of the streets of Rome etc. Young men gained experience, and became known to the people in these posts.

Everyone hoping for a political career had to gain military experience as a junior officer. Relatives or family friends would ask a serving general to accept them as officer trainees. They usually served for 2 to 3 years. Their duties became more important as their experience grew. This was the only military training that future consuls or praetors in command of Rome's armies might have.

Optimates versus populares

Why should the marriage of a fifteen-year-old have been dangerous? The reason was a bitter rivalry which had arisen between two groups in the senate over the last forty or fifty years.

The more powerful group was composed of a comparatively few aristocratic families and their supporters. Most of the consuls over the last 150 years had come from these few families. They resented the growing part played in politics by the tribunes and plebs, which they saw as a threat to their own traditional authority, and opposed any person or new idea which might weaken it. They were known as *OPTIMATES*, which has no equivalent in English, but means something like 'the best men'.

The *POPULARES*, on the other hand, wanted to change the existing situation, largely because they did *not* belong to the powerful families which controlled the senate. Since they were out-voted in the senate, the only way they could make changes was by laws proposed by tribunes and passed in the plebeian assembly, to which the patricians were not admitted.

Marius was a 'popularis'; it was the insistence of the tribunes and plebs that had won him five consecutive consulships, and an army command, against the opposition of the optimates.

The champion of the optimates was Lucius Cornelius Sulla.

Lucius Cornelius Sulla 138–78 BC. From an aristocratic but poor family. We are told that his penetrating stare was made more dreadful by the angry red blotches which covered the pale skin of his face: but none of this shows in any of the surviving likenesses.

Marius and the new army

Marius had been the commander, and Sulla his second-in-command, in the war in Africa (109–104 BC) in which Marius had first become famous. Marius had then won even more fame by destroying two huge Germanic tribes who were trying to march over the Alps and settle in Italy (104–101 BC). To achieve this he had been forced to reorganise the Roman army. By tradition only property-owners could serve in the legions, a legacy of the old days when Roman farmers had proudly insisted on their right to defend their homeland. But this had proved increasingly inefficient, especially in long wars. First, the soldiers were more concerned with returning home than with far-distant conquests. Secondly, in their six years of service – for this became the normal period – the farms often deteriorated so much, despite the efforts of wives and children, that it was impossible or uneconomic to rebuild them. The farmer was left with the choice of signing on again in the army for some other campaign, or joining the mass of unemployed in Rome.

Marius' solution, apart from improving weapons, training and discipline, was to admit to the legions *any* Roman citizen, whether he owned property or not. Thousands of the unemployed volunteered. As a result the army changed from a part-time militia into a permanent force of full-time professional soldiers. But tradition was too strong for Marius to revise the recruitment of the officers. Armies were commanded by praetors or consuls who came from their jobs in Rome to lead the forces in the field. Under them were six *tribuni militum* (military tribunes). These were either young ambitious men seeking the military training thought necessary before a career in politics, or slightly older men who wanted to make their career in the army. The most senior officers, therefore, and the most junior, were more interested in their political careers than in army service.

The trouble with the new army was that the soldiers now had no farms to go back to. Simply to earn their living they were prepared to serve in campaign after campaign. When their service did end they expected their general to persuade the senate to provide them with a plot of land, for there was no official scheme of pensions for ex-soldiers. Consequently the soldiers gave their loyalty to the man in command of them, not to the senate or state. They were willing to follow such a general wherever he led them – even, as we shall see, against Rome itself.

A Roman centurion – the equivalent of a sergeant-major in a modern army. These experienced 'non-commissioned' officers, professional soldiers promoted from the ranks, were vitally important in the Roman army, for the higher officers usually served for only a year or two at a time.

The metal discs (phalerae) on his chest were the Roman equivalent of medals awarded for valour. He carries a vine branch (vitis) as his staff of office. Centurions sometimes used it to beat unlucky soldiers under their command into unconsciousness for some offence.

Civil war in Italy

In 90 BC civil war broke out in Italy. Some of the cities that had been allied to Rome for many generations rebelled and tried to set up an independent state, because the Roman senate kept refusing their claim to full Roman citizenship. (This is known to us as the 'Social War', from *socii*, the Latin word for 'allies'.) Two years' very hard fighting followed. Sulla was given the major command of the war, but Marius was offered only a humiliatingly small part. Peace came, and Italy was reunited, but only when the senate granted the allies' claim to be full citizens of Rome.

This coin, issued by the allies, which shows a bull, the emblem of Italy, goring a she-wolf, the emblem of Rome, is a graphic propaganda announcement of some victory over a Roman army.

Almost immediately war broke out again, this time between Roman and Roman. Sulla, now the consul of 88 BC, was still in command of the army. The senate ordered him to take his troops overseas against Mithridates, king of Pontus, who had invaded the Roman province of Asia and put 80,000 Roman citizens to death. But Marius wanted this command and persuaded the people to transfer it to him. (Remember that a decree of the people in the plebeian assembly had the force of law over all the citizens.) Sulla was furious when he heard the news. He marched the army on Rome and captured the city. The tribune Sulpicius who had given the command to Marius was killed, and Marius had to run away to Africa to save his life. He only avoided capture at one point by burrowing into a heap of dung! Sulla forced the people, overawed by his troops, to give him back the command, and he then took the army off to Asia. The consuls he left behind were Cinna, a popularis, and Octavius, an optimate.

Marius at once returned to Italy, collected an army from his old supporters and joined forces with Cinna. Then he too marched on Rome, defeated Octavius and captured the city. Full of hatred, Marius allowed his troops and slaves to run riot, and they swarmed through the city, murdering and looting. But after five days Cinna was disgusted and used his troops to end the bloodbath. Shortly afterwards, on 1 January 87 BC, Cinna and Marius were declared consuls. Within a few days, fortunately for Rome, Marius died, probably of a heart attack.

Cinna stayed in control for the next three years, being elected consul each year with little trouble, and it was in 84 BC that Caesar married Cinna's daughter Cornelia. Caesar was now firmly in the 'popularis' camp.

Sulla as Dictator

Almost immediately news came that Sulla, after defeating Mithridates, imposing stern peace terms on him and re-organising the province of Asia, was about to return. To spare Italy from another civil war, Cinna began to ship his troops across the Adriatic to face Sulla in Greece. To everyone's dismay, some of Cinna's men, waiting to embark, mutinied and murdered him. Then in 83 BC Sulla did land in Italy with his army. Negotiations with the populares broke down; Sulla fought his way into Rome in 82 BC and his last opponent, Marius' son, committed suicide. Sulla had his enemies hunted down and butchered. Marius' tomb was broken open and his bones thrown into the river. One of Marius' nephews, the praetor Gratidianus, was flogged through the streets: then his arms and legs were smashed with sticks, his ears were cut off, his tongue torn from his mouth and his eyes gouged out. He was still breathing when finally his head was cut off and paraded on a spear. Sulla next posted up 'proscription lists' of nearly 2,000 more victims who were outlawed with a price on their heads. Most of the optimates themselves were horrified by Sulla's savagery, but resistance was impossible: Sulla's army was still garrisoned in Rome.

Then Sulla was declared *Dictator* 'to revise the constitution'. Dictators were appointed only in times of grave emergency. They held office for a maximum of six months, with supreme authority over all other magistrates, and supreme military command. Sulla, however, illegally held the

office for over two years: he passed many laws. Some were fair, designed to uphold justice and order and the authority of the senate. Others were meant to weaken the power of the people. The tribunes, for example, were no longer allowed to introduce legislation in the plebeian assemblies without approval from the senate. Their veto was greatly restricted; they were barred from further office.

Caesar seeks experience

Caesar was too young to take part in any of this. Yet his relationship with Marius, and his marriage to Cinna's daughter, would clearly have aroused Sulla's deepest suspicions. But when he was nineteen, to improve his career chances, someone must have made an approach to the Dictator on Caesar's behalf. He was summoned to Sulla's presence: Caesar, a slim young man, dressed in a loose tunic that was the height of fashion then, faced the most powerful man in the Roman world. Sulla, his face blotched with good living and a scarlet birthmark, was still sharp-eyed and watchful. Caesar was told to divorce Cornelia and marry into an optimate family, to prove his loyalty to the new régime. He went away to think it over. Whatever his reasons – genuine love for Cornelia, his own pride or sense of honour – he refused, and had to run away from Rome. Sulla's troops hunted him down, and caught him: Caesar bought his freedom with a bribe of 12,000 denarii (the denarius was a silver coin, and a legionary soldier at this time was paid 112½ denarii a year, and spent about a third of his pay on his food). At this point members of his family went to Sulla and begged, and obtained, a pardon for him. But Caesar could not stay in Italy. So now he entered on the military service essential for ambitious politicians. As a young aristocrat he became a junior officer under one of his family's friends, the governor of the province of Asia.

The army, the law courts, the pirates

Caesar was still only nineteen when he took part in a successful attack on Mytilene (the leading city-state on the island of Lesbos and one of the last of Mithridates' allies). He won the civic crown ('corona civica') for bravery. We know none of the details, but we do know that this award was given only for

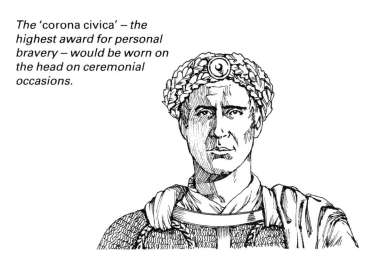

The 'corona civica' – the highest award for personal bravery – would be worn on the head on ceremonial occasions.

saving the life of a comrade in battle. He stayed abroad, continuing his military training until 78 BC, when, hearing of Sulla's death, he returned to Rome.

Ambitious young men often tried to attract attention by a performance in the law courts, and this had been the purpose of Caesar's education. Rome had no public prosecutor, and members of the leading families thought it part of their public duty to bring to court anyone whom they believed to be guilty of crime. The more prominent the defendant, the more fame was to be won by the prosecutor. So in 77 BC and again in 76 BC Caesar launched prosecutions against two of Sulla's dishonest supporters. He was only twenty-three, and quite inexperienced, so it is hardly surprising that he was unsuccessful, especially as some of Rome's leading lawyers spoke against him. However, he worked with such enthusiasm at his speeches that he won a reputation as one of Rome's most promising young orators.

In 75 BC Caesar left Rome for further training in public speaking. One of the most famous teachers of the day, Apollonius Molon, lived in Rhodes, and it was for this island that Caesar set out. But on the way he was captured by pirates and held to ransom. There is a story that on hearing how much they were asking, Caesar exclaimed 'I'm worth much more than that!', and advised them to ask for a much bigger sum. There is no means of knowing whether the story is true or not. But it is true that when the ransom was paid, on his own initiative Caesar raised a squadron of ships, captured several of the pirate vessels and crucified the crews. He was twenty-five.

At last Caesar reached Rhodes. But he had barely set foot ashore when he learned that some of Mithridates' troops had invaded the province of Asia. At once Caesar returned to the mainland, took over command of the local militia and drove the enemy out of the province. Again this action was taken on his own initiative. We know no more details, except that Caesar did not wait for authority from the governor of the province. It is remarkable evidence of Caesar's incredible boldness and self-confidence – and perhaps of the inefficiency of the provincial administration.

In the following year the senate decided to clear the eastern Mediterranean of pirates once and for all. The praetor Marcus Antonius was put in charge of the campaign. Perhaps because of his previous initiative, Caesar was asked to join Antonius' staff. All we know of the campaign is that it was remarkably unsuccessful: when Caesar returned to Rome from Rhodes in 73 BC, in order to avoid the attention of the pirates he had to sail stealthily across the Adriatic in a small boat, accompanied only by two friends and ten slaves.

First steps in office: Caesar becomes military tribune

Caesar's return to Rome did not pass unnoticed: he was beginning to make a name for himself. In 72 BC he was elected to his first public office, one of the twenty-four military tribunates, annually voted by the people's assembly.

About the time he became military tribune, two other men, Marcus Licinius Crassus and Gnaeus Pompeius Magnus, were beginning to dominate Rome's affairs. Crassus had served in Sulla's army and had acquired an enormous fortune by buying up the property of the men outlawed in Sulla's proscription lists. He was now praetor. Pompey (as Pompeius is called in English) had at the age of twenty-four raised a private army to help Sulla, won battles for him in Sicily and Africa, and had since 77 BC been an army commander in Spain.

Now a major crisis threatened Italy: a Thracian gladiator called Spartacus had, in 73 BC, broken out of his training camp in southern Italy, and raised an army, eventually swollen to 70,000 by runaway slaves and others. For two years Spartacus and his desperate men rampaged round Italy, defeating army after army sent against them. Then in 71 BC Crassus was put in charge of the army. He finally trapped and

Gnaeus Pompeius Magnus, 106–48 BC. He was given the cognomen Magnus 'The Great', by Sulla in 81 BC for his help in Sulla's victories. You can see why Cicero called him 'Ox eyes'.

Marcus Licinius Crassus c. 112–53 BC. Far less is known of Crassus than of Pompey or Caesar: he was certainly the richest, and one of the most powerful men in Rome. This bust appears to be the only representation of him that has survived.

destroyed the rebels, crucifying 6,000 of them along the roadside. Pompey, returning with his victorious troops from Spain, then killed the few who had escaped.

Pompey and Crassus, who had never liked each other, now approached Rome with their armies. Using this form of military blackmail, both demanded the consulship of 70 BC. Crassus' claim was perhaps reasonable: he had defeated a dangerous enemy and had been praetor the previous year. But Pompey was six years too young, and had never even been a senator. Yet the senate had to give way. Pompey and Crassus then staged a public reconciliation and dismissed their forces. Though they had both been lieutenants of Sulla they proceeded to sweep away everything that remained of his legislation. Most importantly, they restored to the tribunes all the powers and privileges of which they had been deprived.

Caesar becomes quaestor and senator

In this same year, 70 BC, Caesar was elected as one of the twenty quaestors, a post which allowed him to enter the senate. He was to serve his quaestorship as financial secretary to the province of Further Spain. Before he left Rome, his aunt Julia, Marius' widow, died, and Caesar gave a public funeral speech in her honour. Such speeches were often made in honour of respected citizens, though rarely for women. The long funeral procession would halt in the Forum. One of the relatives would usually mount a rostrum and in glowing terms recall the achievements and character of the dead person and crowds of passers-by would stop and listen. On this occasion the funeral busts of Marius were also displayed, and so Caesar again emphasised his connection with the 'populares'.

When his wife Cornelia died a few weeks later Caesar made another funeral speech in her praise. Never before had such a young woman received this honour, but Caesar had no hesitation in speaking. According to the historian Plutarch, his words 'brought him much sympathy from the people, who regarded him as a tender-hearted man, full of feeling, and liked him for it'. And again Caesar demonstrated his connection with the 'populares', through the consul Cinna, his wife's father. Caesar never missed a chance of winning the attention of the Roman people. He clearly had no thought of a quiet and uneventful future. He then left for Spain.

2 The rise to power, 69–60 BC

Caesar had become quaestor, and thus entered the senate, at the earliest age allowed – thirty. He was also to become aedile and praetor as young as was possible. Unfortunately, we do not know much of what he did in any of these three offices.

Caesar in Spain, 69 BC

As quaestor in Spain in 69 BC, Caesar got on well with the governor, so presumably he carried out his duties to the governor's satisfaction. It is unlikely, though, that the Spaniards were equally pleased. Rome's administration of her provinces was far from honest. The collection of taxes was regarded by a governor and his staff principally as the means to enrich themselves. A fixed sum had to be paid into the treasury at Rome; anything collected above that amount went to the governor, his quaestor and the tax collectors. No real facts at all about Caesar's activities in this province have come down to us. And those stories that have survived – for example, that when Caesar saw a statue of Alexander the Great, he groaned aloud because he had done so little compared with Alexander at the same age – are almost certainly nothing but the result of a later writer's imagination.

On his return from Spain in 68 BC, Caesar married Pompeia, a granddaughter of Sulla. There was no close connection between her family and that of Pompey. It is hard for us to see what the political advantage of this marriage was, but it is almost impossible to believe that the marriage was made for any but a political reason. There was no need for him to marry, for Caesar was never without female friends. Even if he married in the hope of having a son (he already had one daughter, Julia, by his first marriage) the political connection would have been all-important.

Caesar's personal life at this time was notorious, mainly for his extravagance and the number of his affairs with women of

This relief from the Rhineland shows a tax-collector counting the coins spread before him. The payment was recorded in the book on the left of the picture. The carving was made much later in the Empire, when books with pages began to replace rolls, but such a scene, with the bearded provincials queueing in their Celtic duffle coats, cannot have changed much over the centuries.

every age and rank. He had a country house built near Lake Nemi, then had it torn down again when he did not like it. He later gave one of his mistresses, Servilia, the mother of Brutus, a pearl worth 1,500,000 denarii (a year's pay for over 13,000 soldiers!).

It is not surprising, then, that even before entering political life Caesar was said to have had enormous debts. Though he may have enriched himself in Spain, he was going to need an almost unlimited fortune in the near future. A political career in Rome was very expensive. At the elections votes could only be cast by citizens personally present, and the unemployed mob formed a significant proportion of those who actually voted. In order to win their support it had become the normal practice for the candidates to distribute great sums of money in bribes. Despite the attempts of the senate to stamp out such bribery, it had become almost impossible to win an election without it.

Caesar's election campaign: money problems

After Caesar's return from Spain his thoughts must have been on his future. He hoped to become curule aedile as soon as he was eligible, in 65 BC. He would have to work hard to win support. The elections would be held in mid-summer 66 BC, and he would soon have to lay his hands on some ready money for his election campaign.

But there were more than election expenses to be found. The curule aediles were responsible for arranging seven days' games in April and fifteen days' in September. (The plebeian aediles put on a different set of games.) These 'games' were entertainments for public holidays, and consisted of theatrical performances, processions, public banquets and gladiatorial shows. The treasury provided money to cover the basic cost, but ambitious men knew that one of the best ways of winning popularity was to stage really magnificent games and to pay the extra from their own pocket.

This modern artist's impression gives us a good idea of the huge size of the Circus Maximus after its reconstruction by Julius Caesar towards the end of his life, when it seated 250,000 people. Before the Colosseum was built, c. 80 AD, gladiator and beast fights as well as chariot races were held in the Circus.

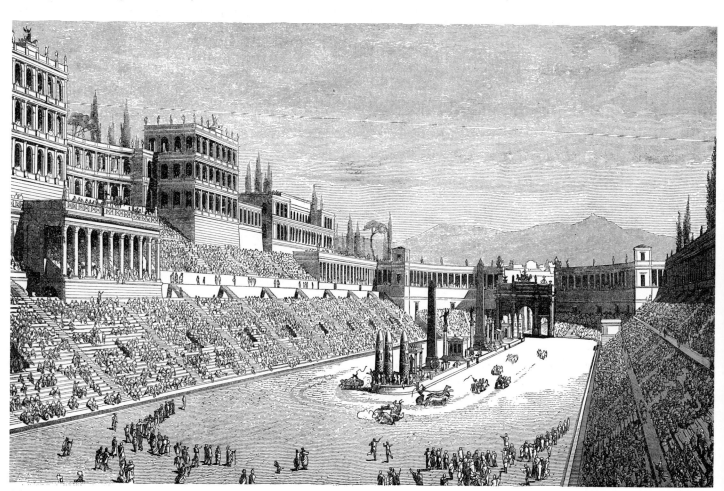

Caesar was easily successful at the elections; but the other man elected as curule aedile was Marcus Bibulus, a rich and obstinate optimate. The two disagreed about almost everything. Together they put on magnificent games: but as we have seen, Caesar knew how to seize the limelight. Bibulus complained, with justice, that he put down all the money and Caesar took all the praise! Furthermore, Caesar also put on funeral games in honour of his father (who had died twenty years before), at which 320 pairs of gladiators fought – the greatest number ever seen up till that time – and won enormous popularity.

Where did all the money come from? Some came from moneylenders. It is easy to see the source of the rest. In 67 and 66 BC Pompey had been given extraordinary commands. First he was sent to rid the Mediterranean of the pirate fleets which infested it (pages 12 and 13), and was spectacularly successful in only 40 days. Secondly he was sent against Mithridates, still a constant menace to Rome's eastern provinces. From 66 BC onward, reports of Pompey's successes poured into Rome, and Crassus' reputation lagged far behind his rival's. So, in order to counter the influence which Pompey would have on his return to Rome, Crassus needed powerful allies. He was one of the first to recognise Caesar's talents. He was also the richest man in Rome, and believed that to help Caesar and so win his friendship would prove a useful investment. So it was with huge loans from Crassus and the normal moneylenders that Caesar was able to win his election to the aedileship, to put on the games he had shared with Bibulus, and to pay for the 320 pairs of gladiators. Caesar was immensely self-confident, and appears to have been unworried about the repayments.

Growing popularity

Many of the optimates looked on Caesar's rise with alarm. They were genuinely disturbed that one man had been able to gather 320 pairs of trained killers in the centre of Rome; it was only a few years since Spartacus' gladiators had terrorised the country. But there was more to come. One night Caesar had the memorials of Marius' victories, which had been taken down by the senate, re-erected in the Forum. The people were delighted to see the gold and bronze glittering in the morning sunlight. But some citizens were less pleased: they were aware

that peaceful government depended on the senate, the magistrates and the people working together, with no one group powerful enough to disregard the others. It was dangerous to upset the balance: they remembered the bloodbath at the time of Marius and Sulla, and wondered how this dazzling young aristocrat would use his popularity. Catulus, one of the leading optimates, was past wondering: the historian Plutarch writes that he declared, 'Caesar is not trying any longer to undermine the republic – he's using the battering rams now!'

Caesar becomes High Priest and praetor

64 BC was a comparatively quiet year for Caesar. 63 BC was very different. First, the *Pontifex Maximus*, or High Priest, died. The office brought with it little real power, but great prestige and a splendid house next to the Temple of Vesta in the Forum. Whatever his religious duties, the High Priest was not prevented from holding other political offices, or even leading armies into battle. Two of the candidates for the office were ex-consuls of great distinction, and convinced optimates; the third was Julius Caesar. Helped by his relationship with Marius, by his many well-known activities as a popularis, and again by huge bribes to the electorate provided by Crassus, Caesar won a sweeping victory. It is unmistakable evidence of Caesar's special qualities that a post normally held only by the most senior and respected men in the state should have gone to such a young man – Caesar was only thirty-six, and still only a candidate for the praetorship elections in July!

Caesar succeeded in this too, and was elected praetor for 62 BC: Bibulus again was one of his colleagues. From now on political events, in which Caesar took no small part, were so dramatic that the historians say nothing about Caesar's routine duties as praetor. Almost at once there began the exciting affair known as 'the Catilinarian conspiracy', a plot to overthrow the government of Rome.

Catiline's conspiracy

'Lucius Sergius Catiline', according to the historian Sallust, 'was of noble birth. He had a powerful intellect and great physical strength, but a vicious and depraved nature. From his

Catiline, under the torrent of Cicero's accusations, is left alone on the benches of the senate house. This is a fresco by Cesare Maccari in the modern Italian senate house. Marcus Tullius Cicero, 106–43 BC, was one of the greatest statesmen and orators of Rome. Many of his speeches and letters have survived, to give us a penetrating insight into Roman politics and the life of famous Roman politicians.

youth he had delighted in civil war, bloodshed, robbery and political strife, and it was in such occupations that he spent his early manhood.' When he returned from the governorship of Africa, Catiline had been prosecuted for taking money from the provincials, and the trial had prevented him from standing for the consulship of 65 and 64 BC. He was even said to be involved in a plot to murder the consuls of 65 BC. He had then been defeated in the elections in July 64 BC (for the consulship of 63 BC), and again in July 63 BC. So he now formed a

conspiracy to overthrow the government by force. He gathered an army of discontented veterans of Sulla's army who had wasted their bounties and then failed to earn a living. The plan was to set Rome on fire and take over the government in the ensuing panic. Suspicions of the plot were revealed in a bold speech by the consul Cicero in the senate. Catiline fled from Rome and joined his army.

Cicero soon found real evidence of the plot and, having arrested five of the conspirators, summoned the senate to discuss their punishment. The first fifteen speakers proposed that they should be executed. Then Caesar suggested that it was a dangerous precedent to execute Roman citizens without a trial. He proposed that they should be imprisoned in strong country towns in Italy instead, that it should be treason for anyone to propose their release, and that their property should be confiscated by the state. Others supported his persuasive speech. But then the tribune Marcus Porcius Cato, a leading optimate, declared his suspicions – Caesar must have proposed such a light punishment because he was himself involved in the plot. When Caesar was given a note as he sat in the senate, Cato challenged him to read it out, expecting it had come from one of the conspirators. Caesar handed it to Cato; it was a love letter from Cato's own half-sister! However, Cato won the day. The conspirators were executed by strangulation. Cicero emerged from the prison and exclaimed 'Dead!' Early in January 62 BC Catiline was killed in battle, fighting against an army led by one of the consuls.

By this time Caesar was praetor. Excitement aroused by the conspiracy gradually dwindled as the months passed. Now people became anxious at the thought of Pompey returning from the east. Would he, like Sulla in 83 BC, also returning from a successful war against Mithridates, lead his army on Rome? Politics in the closing months of the year were dominated by this worry. In December Pompey landed at Brundisium – and to everyone's surprise and relief disbanded his troops and came quietly to Rome. His arrival was overshadowed by news of yet another scandal.

The Clodius affair

Every December, at the house of either a praetor or consul, a ceremony was held one evening to worship an ancient goddess – the *Bona Dea* or 'Good Goddess'. Only women were allowed to attend. So the master left the house, taking with him everything male – even male animals. Then the women prepared the house for the ceremony. This year it was at Caesar's house. Aurelia, his mother, and Pompeia, his wife, were in charge. Suddenly there was a scream from Aurelia's maid: she had discovered a man in disguise! Aurelia at once stopped the ceremony and ordered the doors to be locked. The culprit was found hiding in the room of the slave girl who had let him in. The women rushed home to tell their husbands.

Next morning everyone knew that the guilty man was Clodius, a rich and clever young patrician, already notorious for a string of daring but scandalous exploits. Rumour also said that he was in love with Pompeia, Caesar's wife.

Clodius was prosecuted for sacrilege, though the trial was delayed for months. But Caesar divorced Pompeia at once. He had refused to let himself be summoned as a witness at the trial, saying he knew nothing of Clodius' activities. 'Why divorce your wife, then?' he was asked. 'Because', he replied, 'Caesar's wife must be above suspicion.' Since Caesar himself was, so rumour said, having affairs with the wives of both Crassus and Pompey, and without doubt was heavily involved with Cato's half-sister, there was more than a little cynicism in this remark. Clodius was later released, either because the jury was afraid of the mob which flocked round the court – Clodius was a favourite of the people – or because here too Crassus' money was at work: Crassus probably saw in Clodius, as he had seen in Caesar, a useful and enterprising supporter to counter the enormous prestige of Pompey.

Owing to the trial of Clodius, the allocation of the provinces to be governed by the ex-consuls and ex-praetors had been delayed until March. When the lots were cast Caesar was assigned to Further Spain. But he could not leave immediately. He was of course very heavily in debt, and the moneylenders demanded security before he could depart. Though Crassus was perhaps owed more than anyone else, he still guaranteed a sum of 5,000,000 denarii in Caesar's name. Caesar finally set off in June.

Governor in Spain, 61 BC – victories and riches

Again we know few details of what Caesar did in the province of Further Spain, the western half of Spain. It had not yet been fully incorporated into the Roman empire and was still occupied by warlike tribes who had never been completely subdued and pacified. One ancient author tells us that the part of Spain known as Lusitania was infested with bandits whom Caesar efficiently eradicated. Another says that he marched through the Lusitanians to the Atlantic, subduing hitherto unconquered tribes. A third declares that he sacked several Lusitanian towns, though they had accepted his terms and opened their gates to welcome him, in order to get money to pay off his debts.

Whatever happened, his experiences had a marked effect on him, for he discovered that not only was warfare a fascinating business, but also he was very good at it. Moreover, he returned from Spain a rich man, able to pay off all his debts, and give his troops and the Treasury a lot of money as well. He had also been successful enough in his campaigns to be saluted as *Imperator* by his troops (an honorific title meaning Commander, 'the man who gives the orders', which they gave their generals only after great victories), and the senate awarded him a triumph.

The loss of a triumph

A triumph was the greatest day in any general's life. A huge procession paraded through Rome, including the senate and the magistrates, carts loaded with the loot taken in the war, important prisoners, animals for sacrifice and the general's army. Then at last, amid the cheers of the crowds that packed the streets, came the general himself, standing on a chariot, dressed in a purple and gold toga, with a slave holding a crown above his head.

Caesar was faced with a dilemma. He arrived home in the summer of 60 BC, when the elections for the consulship were about to be held, and he was anxious to be a candidate. The problem was that a general wanting a triumph had to wait *outside* the *pomoerium*, the city boundary, while the arrangements for the triumph were made, but anyone who wanted to be a candidate at the elections had to be present *inside* the city. Polling day had already been announced and, since there was not time enough to hold the triumph beforehand, Caesar asked the senate's permission to offer himself as a candidate while still staying outside Rome, with friends inside the city to canvass for him. The request was refused, mainly through the opposition, again, of Cato. Making a typically quick decision, Caesar crossed the pomoerium, so giving up the triumph. He decided that one day's glory was of no importance at all compared with real power, and he became a candidate for the consulship. He swept in, top of the poll: for the third time in his life he had Bibulus as colleague.

This picture is a scene from a triumph carved on a silver cup found at Boscoreale (buried in the Vesuvius eruption of 79 AD). The triumphant general rides in a chariot, attended by a slave. In front of him march soldiers and captured enemies: an official carrying an axe leads the bulls which he is soon going to sacrifice.

Caesar makes a pact with Pompey and Crassus, 60 BC

Caesar was no doubt aggrieved that he had to give up his triumph. He was not the only one to have suffered at the hands of the optimate group in the senate. When Pompey returned to Italy from the east in 62 BC he could regard himself as the first man in Rome. He had added new provinces to the empire, which more than doubled Rome's income, and celebrated one of the greatest triumphs (his third) which Rome had ever seen. Pompey made two requests of the senate, which must have seemed very reasonable to him: first, that his arrangements in the new provinces should be approved; and second, that land should be made available for his veteran soldiers. The senate was persuaded by the optimate group to allow neither of them.

Normally a group of ten senators should have gone out to the new provinces to draw up details of the settlement. Having conquered all these new lands, Pompey thought he was capable of arranging without any such delay how they should be administered in peace-time as well. He was no doubt right, but his action could be regarded as mere arrogance. In any case the senate was determined to show Pompey that its authority was not to be challenged. It insisted that it should debate every clause of every agreement for every new province. Pompey demanded that they should all be considered together. Despite all the help he could summon from tribunes and consuls, Pompey was unable to make the slightest dent in the senate's stubbornness. Two years after his return from the east, none of his arrangements had been approved, and no land had been granted to his veterans. Pompey was furious.

Crassus, though far less powerful than Pompey, was still the richest man in Rome, with considerable influence. But he too had been snubbed by the senate. Rome had no civil service: administrative tasks, like tax collection, were carried out by private companies, known as *publicani*. The company which had bid for the right to collect the taxes of Asia found that it had undertaken to pay the Roman treasury too much, and asked for the sum to be reduced. Crassus supported the request, but it was turned down by the senate.

Caesar watched and wondered. Pompey and Crassus were far greater men in the state than he was. If the optimates could act like this to them, what could they not do to him? But he

The new provinces added to the empire by Pompey c.62 BC.

was not without power: on 1 January 59 BC, he would be consul. He was aware that Crassus and Pompey were not on speaking terms, but he was determined to negotiate. The backing which each of the three could call upon from his friends and supporters was so strong that, if they could combine into one group, it would be irresistible. All three had been insulted by the senate and had had requests denied. Pompey wanted the confirmation of his settlements in the new provinces, and land for his veterans. Crassus wanted a revision of the Asian tax contract. Caesar, having lost his triumph, now wanted a big military command at the end of his consulship.

Caesar's negotiations were skilful, and successful. A secret pact was agreed between these three men to support each other. This group is now often referred to as the *First Triumvirate*. In the last months of 60 BC it quietly rallied support and prepared to act.

3 The consulship, 59 BC

Suetonius, the author of 'The Twelve Caesars', the lives of the first emperors, wrote this about Caesar as he became consul:

> He was said to have been tall, fair and well built; his face was quite broad, with sharp black eyes . . . he was almost too careful about his appearance, fussy about how his barber cut his hair and shaved him, and some people have alleged he had the surplus hair plucked on other parts of his body. He thought his baldness was ugly, and hated it, especially as his enemies often made fun of it. He often combed his thin hair forward from the crown of his head, and none of the honours granted him by the senate and people pleased him so much as the right to wear a laurel crown on all occasions.

We can imagine he was even more careful than usual about his appearance when he attended his first meeting of the senate as consul. The function of the consuls was to summon and preside over the senate. The senate met, on average, twice a month. Each consul acted as president for a month at a time in turn; Caesar began in January, as he had won most votes. The senate was in practice the main source of law-making and government, for it contained all the men with experience of high office, and a discussion in the senate would produce valuable comments. Though it was possible, with the help of a tribune, to propose new laws in the assembly of the plebs, the senate was a much more suitable place to do so. Therefore, Caesar tried at once to heal the rift between the populares and the optimates.

Caesar's proposal for an agrarian law

In his opening address Caesar declared, 'the consuls must be reconciled, for the good of the state'. He admitted that he was a 'popularis', but said that he intended to act only with the agreement of the senate. Then, in order to fulfil his promises to Pompey, he went on to propose an 'agrarian law', a law by which land was to be distributed to Pompey's veterans, and to other settlers. Money from Pompey's conquests should pay for buying land in Italy at a fair price. The full market price should be paid for any compulsory purchase. When Caesar read out the detailed proposals to the senate he offered to make any improvements suggested. The proposals, and the offer, were so reasonable that the optimates could find no criticisms to make. There could hardly be any doubt that Caesar was making a genuine offer of reconciliation and compromise.

This marble bust of Caesar shows what he looked like at this time. There are many representations of him, made like this one after his death, but based on models made during his lifetime. They are so similar that it is safe to assume that this is a true likeness.

Failure in the senate

When the senate met again to discuss the agrarian bill, Caesar called first on Crassus, and then on Pompey, to speak in favour of it, and so revealed the first signs of the triumvirate's existence; rumour had become fact. Moreover, in calling on

Pompey, Caesar was reminding the senate of the thousands of veteran soldiers the great general could summon to Rome to vote in support of a proposal that offered them their long over-due reward. But when Cato's turn came to speak, he declared, on behalf of the optimate group, that they would allow 'no innovation in the republic'. He then began to use the same tactic by which he had stopped Caesar's request for a triumph – the filibuster. This meant talking non-stop till sunset, when the session automatically ended. This would prevent any further discussion, or voting.

Caesar's temper was always quick, especially when faced with such tactics. He commanded Cato to be quiet. Then, as Cato continued his speech, Caesar ordered an attendant to lead Cato off to prison. The optimates all rose to their feet and followed Cato. 'Where are you going?' called Caesar. 'I prefer', replied one of the praetors, 'to be with Cato in prison rather than here with you.' In giving way to his anger Caesar had revealed that his offer of conciliation, genuine though it might be, was still very fragile. Recovering himself he signal-led to one of the tribunes to let Cato go. Caesar then dismissed the senate. He declared that he would take the bill to the people's assembly, deciding, perhaps too hastily, that he would never be able to carry this piece of legislation through the senate.

Some days later, when the people's assembly had been summoned, Caesar came to the steps of the temple of Castor to propose and explain the bill to the people. Bibulus thrust his way through the Forum with a crowd of supporters. Caesar called on him to support the bill. Even though there was an ancient right for the people to pass laws without the senate's approval, Bibulus cried, 'You shan't have this law this year, not even if you all want it!'. Pompey then spoke, approving of every clause of the bill. Crassus, too, spoke out and gave his support. The people, too, now saw the triumvirate clearly standing against the senate.

Success with the people

On voting day Pompey called his veteran soldiers to Rome to vote: the result could not be in doubt. But Bibulus still opposed the bill. When he tried to make a speech he was jostled by the mob, a bucket of dung was poured over his head, and his *fasces* (bundles of rods) were broken. Three tribunes, trying to block the proposal on behalf of the optimates, were beaten up in a scuffle, and their veto was disregarded. In these unhappy circumstances the bill was passed. Enraged at Bibulus' opposition, an angry tribune tacked on a clause that all the senators should swear an oath to uphold the law after it had been passed.

At the next meeting of the senate Bibulus demanded that the law be abolished on the ground that it had been passed by violence. But the senate, scared by the strong feelings of the people, and by the presence of Pompey's veterans, refused to do so. Moreover, despite strong protests from Cato, the senators one by one took the oath to uphold Caesar's law. Even Cato swore in the end. By April commissioners were hard at work allocating the land.

It has been worth looking at this first action of the year in some detail, for it sheds a grim light on the state of Rome's politics. The events of these dramatic days had a marked effect on the rest of Caesar's life. In disregarding the veto of the tribunes, and, it could be claimed, resorting to mob violence, Caesar had broken the law, even though he had been carrying out the people's wishes. As long as he held an office such as the consulship, or a military command, Caesar could not, by a peculiar rule of Roman law, be brought into court. But if he became a private citizen for one moment, he knew that his enemies would leap to prosecute him. From that day he would be barred from further office and would almost certainly be sent into a humiliating exile. He was determined that this should never happen.

Bibulus versus Caesar

Bibulus now made an extraordinary move in an attempt to hinder Caesar. Following ancient tradition, it was the practice for any consul or praetor presiding over a public assembly to begin by observing the sky. This was to make sure there was no lightning or other bad omen which would mean the meeting would have to be cancelled. Normally this was only a formality, taking a few seconds at most. But now Bibulus declared that he was going to watch the sky for an unlimited period of time, and withdrew to his home to do so. He declared that no public meeting could take place until he came out again. Bibulus stayed at home for the next eight months, and spent his time writing a series of accusations against Caesar. Crowds gathered to read them when they were posted up. Many citizens were now worried about the ease with which Caesar had flouted the senate, disregarded the tribune's veto and, they suspected, organised violence.

But Caesar pressed on with the other laws he had planned. He was not going to be stopped by what he regarded as Bibulus' ludicrous antics. Most of his laws were carried in the people's assembly, though our sources often fail to tell us where the proposals were made. We do know that some measures were proposed and discussed in the senate, and that the optimate group let them pass, gloomily aware that Caesar would only take them to the people if they did not.

Roman officials had constantly to be on guard for ill omens, either by watching the sky for signs like lightning or the flight of birds, or by inspecting the entrails of sacrificed animals like the bull in this ancient sculpture. They believed that the approval or disapproval of the gods could be divined from the colour, size and position of the liver, for example.

New laws and proposals

For Crassus and Pompey

The Asian tax contract was reduced as Crassus had asked, so that the publicani, the private tax-collecting companies, had to deliver only two-thirds of the sum they had originally undertaken to pay to the treasury. Caesar did warn them to be more careful about their contracts in the future – which many took as a cynical joke.

Pompey's arrangements in the eastern provinces were also approved. This was sensible, for there was nothing wrong with the arrangements themselves, only with the way he had disregarded the senate in making them. Now the requirements of both Pompey and Crassus were fully satisfied.

For the unemployed

Another agrarian bill allocated state-owned land in Campania, normally leased to rich tenants, to over 20,000 of the unemployed in Rome. By this measure Caesar was doing something to solve real social problems in Italy, for no one could doubt that some provision for the poor and unemployed was desperately needed. At the same time he and Pompey, who was associated with Caesar in the proposal, won for themselves another 20,000 loyal supporters; it was mainly for this reason that the optimates opposed the bill.

For foreign affairs

There were also foreign relations to be considered. Ariovistus, a German chief living in Gaul, was recognised as a 'friend of the Roman people'. Reports had reached Rome that Ariovistus had been invited into an alliance with some Gallic tribes which were enemies of Rome, and it seems possible that Caesar was trying to detach him from that alliance. He may have had other motives, as we shall see in the next chapter – we cannot be certain. But we do know why Caesar pushed through a proposal that Ptolemy should be recognised by Rome as the lawful king of Egypt: Pompey and Caesar shared a gift of 36,000,000 denarii from the grateful king.

For better government

Not all Caesar's new measures were dictated by thoughts of his own advantage. He arranged that every day there should

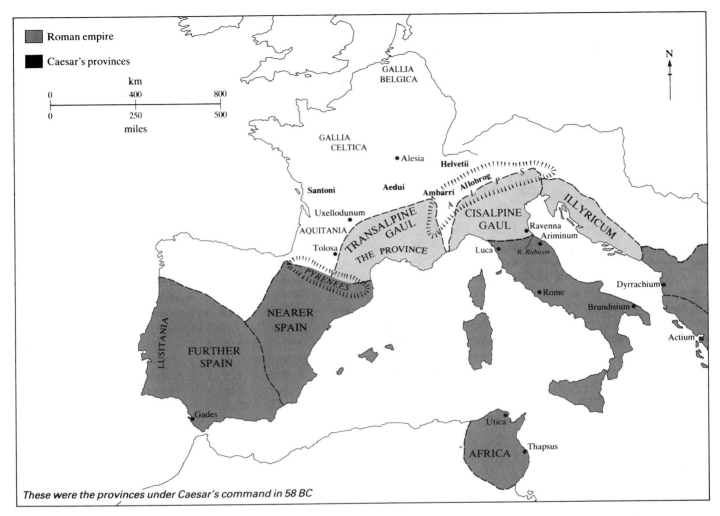

These were the provinces under Caesar's command in 58 BC

be posted up in the Forum copies of the people's assembly's laws, resolutions of the senate, or other items of important news. These *acta diurna* (daily proceedings), a sort of 'official gazette', were also copied and circulated even in the provinces.

Later in the year, he drafted a bill, with over a hundred clauses, completely overhauling the administration of the provinces. This was an act of genuine reform. As we have seen, the governors of provinces were notorious for their dishonesty, and Caesar himself had enriched himself in Spain. Cicero, in a speech he made some years earlier, had summed

the situation up: 'All the provinces are in mourning: there isn't a place which hasn't been invaded by the greed and injustice of our fellow-countrymen' and 'It is difficult to find words to express the extent of the hatred in which we are held by foreign nations.' This was what Caesar set out to cure.

But in May Caesar took steps to provide for his own future. A bill was passed in the people's assembly which gave Caesar his next command, the provinces of Cisalpine Gaul and Illyricum, together with three legions, for a period of five years. The senate was, to its dismay, excluded from the whole affair. When the governor of Transalpine Gaul died suddenly,

25

the senate, on the proposal of Pompey, added this province and another legion as well. It may seem extraordinary that the senate should have increased the power of a man that most of them distrusted and loathed. Indeed, Cato, as usual, spoke out openly against it. But they were afraid that if they resisted, the people would yet again be given the chance to interfere in what really should have been the senate's business. Moreover, they felt that the Roman territory in Gaul, and even perhaps north Italy itself, was likely soon to face real danger, and Caesar had proved his military competence in Spain.

The triumvirate under strain

Though the triumvirs – Caesar, Pompey and Crassus – had gained what they wanted, they were increasingly uneasy. The vigour and ruthlessness with which laws were forced through, and especially the way in which the tribunes' veto and Bibulus' authority as a consul were constantly flouted, had made the three hated in the senate and unpopular with many of the citizens. Caesar knew that Pompey genuinely disapproved of his methods. To make sure of his support, Caesar arranged in April that his attractive daughter, Julia, should marry Pompey. (Though there was a difference of thirty years between them, and though the marriage had purely political motives, it proved a very happy match.) Soon Caesar himself remarried. His bride was Calpurnia, the daughter of one of the candidates for the consulship of 58 BC.

These marriages made many citizens even more worried, as they saw Caesar's personal ambitions becoming more and more obvious. They still feared that Pompey might rely on his veteran troops and, like Sulla, use them to seize Rome. As for Crassus, he was too rich, and was owed too much money by too many men. Even the mob of the unemployed, who now dominated the people's assembly, were worried. In midsummer Bibulus was able, by a decree issued from his house, to postpone the consular elections until October – the men likely to top the polls were firm supporters of Caesar, and Bibulus hoped that there might be a change in the three months he had gained. When Caesar tried to lead the people to Bibulus' house, to persuade him to stop the decree, they refused to leave the Forum.

Caesar was safe from prosecution as long as he held office, but Crassus and Pompey were anxious about what would happen as soon as he left for Gaul. If they lost control of the people's assembly completely, the optimate group might be able to have their laws annulled. And Caesar, suspecting that Pompey, besides disapproving of his methods, was also jealous of his success, was afraid that the optimates might still be able to win him over, despite his marriage to Julia.

So it was at this time that Caesar dealt with the long bill reforming provincial administration, to make it clear that he was aiming at the public good, not private advantage. Meanwhile a bill was passed in the people's assembly by which 5,000 poor citizens were to be settled in an existing colony at Comum in Cisalpine Gaul. Caesar personally saw to the settling of these citizens over the next twelve months. By this measure Caesar not only strengthened his position in Rome, but also gained supporters in a province he was to govern at the end of the year.

When the consular elections eventually came in October, Bibulus' delaying tactics failed. The triumvirate, by use of the strength of their supporters, and Crassus' money, were able to ensure that their friends, Aulus Gabinius and Lucius Calpurnius Piso, were elected consuls. When Cato complained in the people's assembly that Gabinius had employed illegal methods in his canvassing, and called Pompey a dictator, he was almost killed by the mob. On the other hand some energetic optimates were elected praetors. Two of them, as soon as they entered office in 58 BC, began a formal debate in the senate about Caesar, and proposed that all his acts as consul should be declared invalid on the grounds that they had been passed illegally.

Caesar declared himself ready to submit to the judgement of the senate. He could after all point to his very first act, the agrarian law, and emphasise that all the senators, Cato included, had sworn to uphold it. But when after three days the senators were still discussing the matter, he decided to wait no longer. Putting on his general's scarlet cloak he left the city, crossed the pomoerium, and so formally entered on his command. He was now a general in charge of an army. Almost at once news from Gaul called him urgently to his province.

4 The Gallic War, 58–50 BC

The news that reached Caesar was that the Helvetii were planning to migrate from Switzerland, through his province of Transalpine Gaul, into the south-west of free Gaul. Gaul was a huge country. Its people were a mixture of races, skilled in agriculture, mining and metallurgy. The tribes traded along their extensive river system, and minted their own gold coins. Caesar believed that a warlike tribe like the Helvetii was bound to cause 'violence and destruction' on its march, and that it would be a constant danger to his province if it settled in south-west Gaul.

So he hurried to Geneva: he arrived in 8 days, averaging 145 kilometres (90 miles) a day. On his way he collected the legion in Transalpine Gaul and as many extra soldiers as he could, and had the bridge over the Rhône at Geneva destroyed. The Helvetii asked for permission to pass through the province: Caesar told them to return for an answer in two weeks:

> In the meantime, with the legion I had with me and the troops gathered from the Province, I had a wall built, 16 feet high, and a ditch, for the 19 miles [30 kilometres] from Lake Geneva to Mount Jura . . . When this earthwork was finished, I put forts and garrisons along it, so that it would be easier to stop them if they tried to force a crossing.
> (*Commentaries on the Gallic War*, book I, chapter 8)

Such speed and resolute action was to be typical of everything Caesar did over the next ten years in Gaul. And by 50 BC he had added Gaul to the empire as Rome's largest province, slaughtering hundreds of thousands of its people in the process. He had no authority to do so: his assault was not provoked, and he could not pretend his actions were defensive. He was aiming at conquest for Rome's sake, and his own.

Though Caesar was busy campaigning every year in the summer months, when food for his men could be taken from the land, he spent most winters in Cisalpine Gaul. Here he was near enough to keep an eye on affairs in Rome, and, too, on Pompey and Crassus, in case their loyalty should waver. He could not afford to be 'out of sight, out of mind', or to be without power and influence when he did eventually return to Rome.

He found an ideal way to justify his exploits in Gaul, to advertise his achievements, and so to keep himself in the public eye. He proved to be a talented author as well as one of the greatest generals of all time. Every winter he wrote a book or commentary, on the year's activities. Some historians think that he had it copied and distributed every spring, to make a fresh impact on the Roman public each year. Others believe that he only had the whole collection published in 51 BC, when he particularly needed to influence the senate. We cannot now be certain; in any case the Commentaries were admired then (particularly by Cicero), and have been ever since.

Though Caesar followed ancient custom and wrote about himself in the third person, the translations from his book in this chapter have, in modern practice, used the first person 'I'. Extracts from Caesar's account of the campaigns in Gaul are related below, in yearly sections, as they are in his Commentaries.

Caesar defeats the Helvetii, 58 BC

When the Helvetii did try to cross into Gaul, Caesar drove them off. He summoned the other three legions from his province, conscripted two new ones, and gave chase. A quarter of the Helvetii were killed before they could cross the river Saône (A) (see map on page 28). Caesar then built in one day a bridge across the river to pursue the others. He utterly defeated them in a battle (B) three weeks later, and sent the 110,000 that survived from the original 368,000, back to Switzerland to stop any migrant German tribes moving in.

Caesar was then asked by some Gauls to deal with Ariovistus, a German chief who had brought his tribe over the Rhine (page 24); they had settled amongst the Sequani and helped them attack and defeat the Aedui, who were allies of Rome.

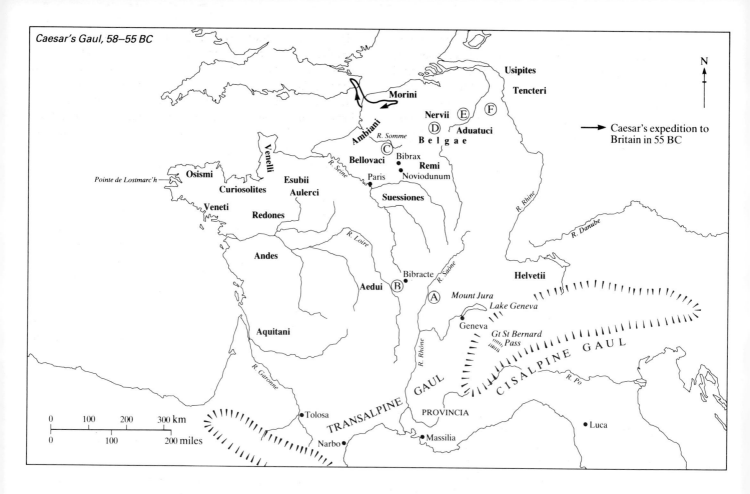

Caesar's Gaul, 58–55 BC

→ Caesar's expedition to Britain in 55 BC

Ariovistus refused when told to depart, and chose to fight (C). Only he and a few others lived to escape across the Rhine; he died soon afterwards.

Leaving the six legions in winter quarters, Caesar went back to Cisalpine Gaul. His first year had been a great success: he had routed the dangerous Helvetii invaders, and was firmly established in Gaul.

Caesar describes his problems in pursuing the Helvetii

Every day I kept asking the Aedui [allies of the Romans] for the corn which their government had promised. For because of the cold – Gaul, as I have said, is a northern country – the corn in the fields was not ripe, and there was not much hay either. Nor could I use the corn brought up the Saône in boats, because the Helvetii had turned away from the river, and I did not want to lose contact with them. (*Commentaries on the Gallic War*, book I, chapter 16)

Caesar's part in the victory over the Helvetii: superior equipment

I sent all the officers' horses out of sight, beginning with mine, so that everyone might be in the same danger, and no one have any hope of escape. I encouraged the men and joined battle. As they were throwing their javelins from

28

higher ground our soldiers easily shattered the enemy formation, then drew their swords and charged them. It was a great handicap to the Gauls in the fighting that several of their shields could be pierced and pinned together by a single javelin, which could not be tugged out because its head had bent. With their left arms encumbered they could not fight properly; many of them, after repeatedly trying to pull their arms free, preferred to drop their shields and fight unprotected. At last, exhausted by their wounds, they begin to retreat to a hill about a mile away [1.6 km]. (*Commentaries on the Gallic War*, book I, chapters 24–5)

Caesar overruns northern Gaul, 57 BC

Conscripting another two new legions, Caesar marched north in the spring, to demonstrate the power of Rome among the Belgae. Several tribes attacked the Romans; they were routed (C) and surrendered. Caesar won another victory against the Nervii (D), in which he escaped defeat and death only by a hair's breadth. The Aduatuci submitted, but made a surprise night attack (E): 4,000 were killed and 53,000 sold into slavery as punishment for treachery.

Caesar relied on diplomacy as well as force: the Remi learnt that friendship with Rome could help them dominate their neighbours, and asked for an alliance which Caesar was glad to grant. When Crassus' son, Publius, was sent round the north-west coast with one legion, the Veneti, Venelli, Osismi, Curiosolites, Esubii, Aulerci and Redones all submitted willingly.

Gaul appeared to have been won. But Caesar carefully placed the legions' winter quarters among the tribes recently overcome, and one was stationed to guard the road to Italy over the Great St Bernard Pass.

In Rome even the senate joined in the surge of national pride at Caesar's achievements, which nearly cancelled out his earlier unconstitutional behaviour, and voted an unprecedented 15-day thanksgiving.

Caesar describes the battle against the Nervii

I made my way to the right wing and found the troops in trouble: the cohorts of the twelfth legion had become so tightly packed together that the men were getting in one another's way as they fought. All the centurions of the fourth cohort, as well as the standard-bearer, had been killed, and the standard was lost. Nearly all the centurions of the other cohorts had been killed or wounded, including the very brave senior centurion P. Sextius Baculus, who had so many terrible wounds that he could no longer stand up. The rest of the men were getting slower, and some in the rear had stopped fighting, and were running away to avoid the spears of the enemy, who kept pouring up the hill and were closing in on both flanks.

I saw that the situation was critical, as there were no reserves available. Snatching a shield from a soldier in the rear rank, for I had come without one, I ran forward to the front line. Calling to the centurions by name, and encouraging the other soldiers I told them to spread out so that they could use their swords more effectively. Their hopes and courage were renewed by my arrival, and every man, with his general looking on, was keen to do his best at whatever personal risk, and the enemy attack was slowed down a little.
(*Commentaries on the Gallic War*, book II, chapter 25)

Two more legions, marching some way behind, at last appear on the scene.

Their arrival changed everything. Even the men who had fallen to the ground from the severity of their wounds propped themselves on their shields and started fighting again. The camp servants, even though they were unarmed, turned to face the enemy; the cavalry, anxious to wipe out the disgrace of running away earlier by their courage now, were everywhere trying to outshine the legionaries.

But the enemy, even in their desperate plight, showed enormous courage; when their front rank fell, those behind stood on their bodies to fight. When they too fell the survivors kept hurling their spears from the top of the pile of corpses, and flung our javelins back at us. One cannot help regarding them as men of the highest courage, whose fighting spirit made light of such difficulties.
(*Commentaries on the Gallic War*, book II, chapter 27)

Winter 57–56 BC: politics in Rome

But the news from Rome was not all good. Clodius, tribune for 58 BC, whom Caesar had 'hired' to protect his interests, had gone too far. He had exiled Cicero (for his execution of the Catilinarians), enacted the *free* distribution of corn to all citizens, and humiliated Pompey. Pompey had arranged the recall of Cicero to support him. When a great shortage of corn, caused partially by Clodius' free distributions, led to rioting in the streets, Pompey was given a special five-year command, with an army, to overhaul the corn supply. Pompey seemed to be growing independent of the triumvirate, and Cicero was openly working to break it up.

Caesar could not afford to let this happen. A bitter opponent, Lucius Domitius Ahenobarbus, was likely to be elected consul for 55 BC, declaring that he would have Caesar recalled. Caesar had other needs too, which only the triumvirate could satisfy. He could not leave his province, so in April 56 BC Pompey and Crassus joined him at Luca, the southernmost town in Cisalpine Gaul.

Caesar, Pompey and Crassus reached a new agreement. This was gradually revealed over the following months. To neutralise Ahenobarbus, Crassus and Pompey were themselves to become the consuls of 55 BC. Caesar would send home some troops on leave to ensure that the elections went as planned. After their consulship they too were to be given five-year commands, Pompey in Spain and Crassus in Syria. Caesar's command was to be extended for another five years. All these commands would end at the close of 50 BC. Caesar was also to be consul again in 48 BC after the ten-year gap between consulships required by law (no one was to be allowed to propose that a successor should be sent to Gaul; in this way Caesar might remain in his province till 48 BC, free from the fear of prosecution).

These were the main points of the agreement; the three men had callously swept aside all normal constitutional arrangements; it is no wonder that later Roman historians believed that this triumvirate marked the end of the republic.

56 BC: revolt on the north-west coast

Over the winter, the tribes of north-western Gaul began to regret their hasty submission to Caesar. So they rebelled, arresting the Roman envoys who came to requisition corn. Caesar ordered a fleet to be built on the River Loire, and returned to Gaul in the spring to crush the rebels. Sending his lieutenants to keep the rest of Gaul under control, he advanced on the strongest and most warlike tribe, the Veneti. But he had no success against the tribe's coastal forts, until the new fleet arrived and defeated their great ships. When they submitted, every member of their council was executed and the whole tribe was sold into slavery. Caesar claimed that his envoys demanding corn were really ambassadors, and that the Veneti had broken international law by arresting them. He wanted an excuse for his savage treatment, which he hoped would terrify the rest of Gaul.

How the rebellion of the coastal tribes broke out

> When these operations (in 57 BC) were over I had every reason to think that Gaul was pacified – the Belgae had been overcome, the Germans driven out and the Alpine

This promontory, surrounded by cliffs, and with its narrow neck blocked by ditches and ramparts, is typical of the strongholds of the Veneti, and shows why Caesar had so much trouble in overcoming them. It is at Points de Lostmarc'h, near the Bay of Douarnez.

tribes subdued. In the winter I set out for Illyricum, wanting to visit its tribes and find out what it was like. But suddenly war broke out in Gaul; this was the reason. Young Publius Crassus and the seventh legion were in winter quarters amongst the Andes, near the Atlantic. Because there was a corn shortage in that area he had sent various auxiliary and legionary officers to the neighbouring tribes – including the Esubii, Curiosolites and Veneti – to get food.

The Veneti are by far the most powerful tribe on this coast: they have the largest fleet of ships, in which they trade with Britain, and in sailing they outclass everyone else in skill and experience. The sea on that coast is open and rough; the Veneti control the few harbours, and so can collect a toll from anybody using those waters.
(*Commentaries on the Gallic War*, Book III, chapter 8)

How the Roman fleet was successful against the enemy's much larger ships

> Our men had prepared one piece of equipment, which proved very useful, sharp-pointed hooks firmly fixed on long poles, similar to the grappling hooks used in sieges. With these they grabbed the ropes holding the yards to the masts, pulled them tight, then snapped them by suddenly rowing hard away. When this happened the yards, of course, fell down; since the Gallic ships relied entirely on sails and their rigging, as soon as they lost them they were quite unable to manoeuvre . . . our ships pursued them, one by one, and captured them."

(*Commentaries on the Gallic War*, book III, chapters 14–15)

55 BC: Caesar exterminates two whole tribes, then crosses the Rhine and the Channel

In 55 BC two German tribes, the Usipites and Tencteri, came over the Rhine. They asked to be allowed to stay in Gaul, but Caesar refused permission. During negotiations, their cavalry attacked and routed Caesar's cavalry. When the German leaders came to apologise, Caesar arrested them, marched to their unsuspecting camp (F) (see p.28), and butchered all 430,000 men, women and children.

Caesar then crossed the Rhine, about 300 metres wide (328 yards), by a wooden bridge built in only ten days. He burnt the villages, buildings and crops, then returned, destroying the bridge behind him.

This appalling example of terrorist tactics, followed by an extraordinary feat of engineering, demonstrates a bizarre mixture of qualities in Caesar and his army.

Caesar visits Britain

In the late summer of 55 BC an expedition was made to explore Britain. It was almost a disaster. A storm damaged Caesar's ships at anchor; a legion was ambushed while collecting food, and only rescued in the nick of time. Caesar accepted peace terms, but sailed back at night, not even waiting for the hostages he had demanded.

Caesar interrupts his description of the battle with this admiring account of the Britons

> In chariot fighting, the Britons first drive all over the field hurling javelins; their enemy are usually scared and confused by the horses and the noise of the wheels. Then, after threading through their own cavalry squadrons, they jump down from the chariots and fight on foot. Meanwhile the drivers withdraw a little from the fighting, positioning the chariots so that their masters can easily retreat to their own lines if they are hard pressed by the enemy's numbers. Thus they combine the mobility of cavalry and the steadfastness of infantry. By daily training and practice they are so skilled that even on a steep slope they can control the horses at full gallop, and check and turn them in a moment, or run along the pole, stand on the yoke and instantly get back into the chariot.

(*Commentaries on the Gallic War*, book IV, chapter 33)

Neither of these ventures into Germany and Britain had been necessary, but Caesar was adventurous and inquisitive. The Roman public was greatly impressed by these journeys to mysterious lands, and the senate voted a 20-day thanksgiving. But many Romans were equally appalled by Caesar's brutality.

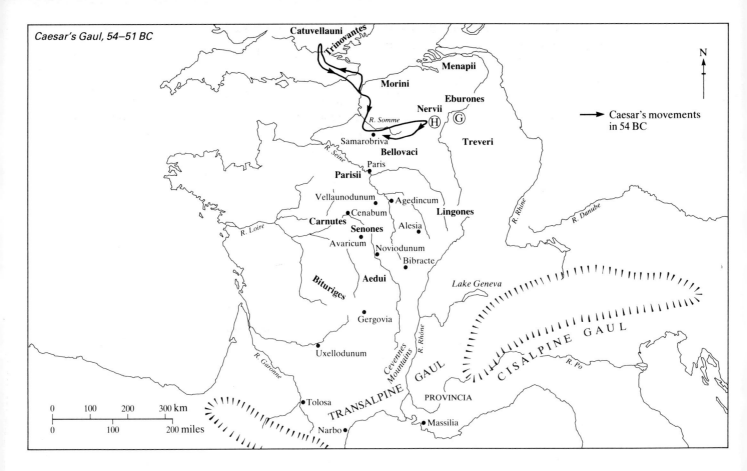

Caesar's Gaul, 54–51 BC

Caesar describes the Britons

The interior of Britain is inhabited by people who, according to their own traditions, originated there . . . the population is very large; there are many buildings, much like those in Gaul, and great numbers of cattle. They use bronze or gold coins, or iron bars of a fixed weight instead of coins. Tin is found inland, a little iron near the coast. They use imported bronze. There is timber of every kind, as in Gaul, except beech and fir. They do not think it right to eat hares, chickens or geese, but rear them as pets. The climate is more temperate than Gaul's, and the winter is less severe.

Most of the people in the interior do not sow corn, but live on milk and meat and wear clothes of animal skin. They all dye themselves with woad, which makes them blue and

54 BC: the second invasion of Britain and revolt in Gaul

Caesar alleged that the Gauls were receiving help from Britain. He decided on a second, much stronger, expedition. He crossed the Channel with 5 legions and 2,000 cavalry in 600 ships (built during the winter by his troops' marvellous enthusiasm), and this time he achieved some military and diplomatic success. Though his fleet was again damaged, he defeated some major tribes led by Cassivellaunus of the Catuvellauni, who mustered 4,000 war-chariots. He made an alliance with the Trinovantes and others, took hostages, and fixed a yearly tribute (payment) to be sent to Rome.

gives them a wild appearance in battle. They wear their hair long, and shave every part of the body except the head and upper lip. Wives are shared between groups of ten or twelve men, usually brothers, or fathers and sons: the children are reckoned to belong to the man the woman first slept with.
(*Commentaries on the Gallic War*, book V, extracts from chapters 12–14)

On his return to Gaul, Caesar was again faced with rebellion. A grain shortage had forced him to place his winter quarters widely apart. All were attacked, though luckily never at the same time. One winter camp holding 1½ legions was wiped out with its two legionary commanders by the Eburones (G), and another (H) was besieged. Only strong action by Caesar and his other commanders prevented disaster. Even then the situation was so tense that Caesar dared not risk leaving Gaul, and stayed at Samarobriva for the winter.

53 BC: Caesar's vengeance

Caesar determined to spread terror throughout Gaul by savage punishment of the rebellious Eburones. He first recruited three more legions in Cisalpine Gaul to replace the 1½ he had lost. Then, even before winter was over, four legions marched against the Nervii. Vast numbers of men and cattle were captured, and handed over as loot to the legions. When the Senones, Carnutes and Treveri refused to send envoys to him, he treated this as open rebellion. He caught the Senones by surprise and they and the Carnutes submitted. Labienus and three legions defeated the Treveri. Caesar overran the Menapii, and crossed the Rhine again to scare off the Germans. At last he turned on the Eburones, who had destroyed the legionary camp. He systematically plundered and devastated their country. He burnt every village and building and consumed all their crops. Nothing was left for the Eburones; the tribe was completely wiped out, and never heard of again. Returning to the Senones, he had their unsuspecting chief tried and executed. Six legions were quartered on Agedincum, their capital, two among the Treveri, two with the Lingones. Absolute quiet reigned in Gaul.
Caesar returned to Cisalpine Gaul for the winter.

52 BC: the great rebellion

Revolt flared in central Gaul. Caesar hurried with new recruits, first to push back a diversionary raid into the province ordered by the chief, Vercingetorix, whom the Gauls had chosen to lead their revolt, then over the Cevennes mountains through snow drifts over two metres high (six feet). He managed to avoid Vercingetorix and he joined the army at Agedincum. When Caesar took the fortified settlements of Vellaunodunum, Cenabum and Noviodunum, Vercingetorix inspired his followers to adopt a 'scorched earth' policy which nearly starved the Roman army. But Caesar stormed Avaricum, where only 800 out of 40,000 men, women and children survived. He sent Labienus against the Senones and Parisii, but at Gergovia he suffered his first major defeat. Fortunately Labienus had won a great victory near Paris, and with his help Caesar drove Vercingetorix into the hill-town of Alesia. Caesar built two rings of earthworks, one to keep Vercingetorix in, the other to repel the Gallic force trying to relieve him. Though 240,000 strong, it failed to break Caesar's siege. To save his people Vercingetorix surrendered; he was led in Caesar's triumph in 46 BC and then executed. It had been a bitter struggle. Caesar wintered in Bibracte: the senate voted a 20-day thanksgiving.

The impressive qualities of Vercingetorix and the Gauls

After this series of disasters at Vellaunodunum, Cenabum and Noviodunum, Vercingetorix summoned a council, and showed that their campaign must be completely changed: 'We must do everything possible to prevent the Romans getting food or fodder. This will be easy, because we are strong in cavalry, and the season is in our favour: there is no grass to be cut, so the enemy will have to send out foraging parties in search of hay in barns. Our cavalry can go out every day and wipe these parties out. Our lives are in danger; we must sacrifice personal property. Every village, every farm must be burnt along the Roman line of march, for as far as their foragers can possibly reach. We have plenty of supplies . . . the Romans will starve, or run great risks by venturing too far from camp . . . We must also set on fire any fortified town whose defences or position do not make it absolutely safe, in case our shirkers go and hide in them, or the Romans loot their supplies of food and wealth. These measures may seem harsh and cruel; but how much worse to have your wives and children made slaves and yourselves killed, which is bound to happen if you are conquered!

This plan was unanimously approved, and 20 towns of the Bituriges were burnt in a single day. Other tribes did the same, until fires were visible in every direction. Though they were all greatly distressed, they comforted themselves with the thought that victory was guaranteed and would restore all they had lost.
(*Commentaries on the Gallic War*, book VII, chapters 14–15)

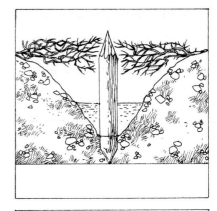

The lilies and goads mentioned by Caesar looked like this.

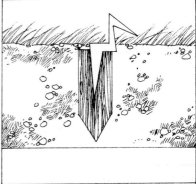

The equally impressive determination of Caesar and his men

Our siegeworks [at Alesia] were 11 miles [17½ kilometres] in circuit, with camps at strategic points, and 23 forts manned by day and night in case of a sudden attack. I had a trench dug 20 feet [6 metres] wide, with straight sides, as wide at the bottom as the top. 400 yards [366 metres] behind this two more trenches were dug, of equal depth and 15 feet [4½ metres] wide; the inner one, on the low ground of the plain, was filled with water diverted from a stream. Behind these was a palisaded rampart 12 feet [3.6 metres] high, to which I added a breastwork with battlements, and where the breastwork joined the rampart large forked branches projected, to stop anyone trying to climb up. Along the entire circuit towers were placed at every 130 feet [40 metres].

In front of these defences, trenches 5 feet [1½ metres] deep were dug, in the bottom of which were sunk five rows of interlaced tree trunks or large branches, stripped of bark and sharpened to a point, with just the tops projecting; anyone entering these trenches was impaled on the sharp points. The soldiers named them 'tombstones'. In front of these were diagonal rows of pits, 3 feet [1 metre] deep, with sharpened stakes in the bottom; their points were concealed with twigs and brushwood: these were called 'lilies' by the soldiers. In front of these again were blocks of wood a foot long in which iron hooks were fixed. These were scat-

tered thickly everywhere, and sunk into the ground: the soldiers called them 'goads'.

Another similar triple line of defences, 14 miles [22½ kilometres] long, was built outside the first ring to protect the troops from attacks from outside.
(*Commentaries on the Gallic War*, book VII, chapters 72–5, with omissions)

51–50 BC: the pacification of Gaul

The concluding book of the Commentaries was written after Caesar's death by his secretary, Aulus Hirtius. Aware that Caesar's command might soon end, some tribes fought on in 51 BC. Order was quickly restored among the Bituriges, but the Bellovaci put up a long and severe resistance before surrendering, and Caesar once more devastated the land of the Eburones to make resurgence impossible. His lieutenants secured the loyalty of the Treveri and the tribes in Normandy, Brittany and round the Loire. Caesar toured extensively to reassure the inhabitants by his mercy – a gesture as calculated as his previous cruelty. Finally, some determined rebels from many tribes took refuge in the hill-fort at Uxellodunum, and held out till Caesar diverted the water supply: the captives had their right hands cut off, 'so that everyone could see how criminals were punished'.

The rest of the year and the next were devoted to restoring Gaul to health. Nearly a third of the men able to bear arms had been killed, another third had become prisoners or slaves. 800 places had been captured, many ruined in the process. Huge areas of land had been plundered or devastated. Gaul was now divided into three provinces, and separate agreements were drawn up between each tribe and Rome. Many tribesmen who had stayed loyal, or who now formed the pro-Roman local government, were rewarded with Roman citizenship. The name Julius, which these new citizens adopted, became widespread. A small tribute was imposed, and the Gauls themselves were allowed to collect it.

Caesar had tried to terrorise the Gauls into submission. He came to realise that the appalling cruelty with which he had ordered hundreds of thousands of his Gallic enemies to be brutally slaughtered or maimed had only served to arouse them to greater hostility. His behaviour alarmed some of the Romans, who dreaded his return to Rome, fearing that he would treat his Roman enemies with similar ferocity. From now on, at any rate, he displayed towards his enemies a moderation as remarkable as his former savagery.

From a modern standpoint we can see that Caesar's success was only due to the disunity of the Gauls; together they could easily have massacred his ten legions. But if the Romans had not taken over the country, then the Germans might have done so instead. The higher Roman standard of living, the roads and fine buildings, the vigorous trade and manufacture, the system of law and all the other marks of civilisation that Gaul gained from the Romans, would only have come centuries later and in another form. As it was, one generation of Gauls was ruthlessly destroyed, but subsequent generations enjoyed peace and prosperity.

Caesar's conquest of Gaul is a vital factor in world history. Mediterranean culture flooded into north-western Europe, guarded by the frontier of the Rhine, which Caesar had fixed. Modern France is a Latin country, and Caesar was its founder.

The Commentaries on the Gallic War

Caesar's year-by-year accounts contain only his own view of what happened. They were written to impress the Roman public, who were expected to marvel both at the difficulties which Caesar had, for their sake, overcome, and at the heroism of the legions in the face of a dangerous and always numerically superior enemy. They may gloss over Caesar's failings or omit what he did not want to be known; they may contain mistakes and exaggerations. They *were* written to plead Caesar's cause. But the first readers included men who had fought in his army, and countless Romans who had corresponded with and questioned his officers. If he had told downright lies to enhance his own name, the lies would have been spotted and his reputation immediately ruined. Caesar was not stupid.

One fact he did not mention. The wealth which Caesar brought back from Gaul was quite enormous. His rewards to his troops were constantly generous. He spent huge sums for political purposes, to win supporters. He spent money like water, both in Rome and in the provinces, on buildings which were intended to win him popularity. The land alone for the new Forum Julium which he was building in Rome had cost 25,000,000 denarii (Caesar's soldiers were paid 225 denarii a year, and Cicero's fine house in a fashionable quarter of Rome cost 250,000 denarii). Most of his riches came from the plundering of Celtic shrines, where pious offerings had piled up over the centuries. Gold flooded into Italy in such a torrent that it fell to two-thirds of its previous value.

But Caesar's political future, on which his life depended, had still to be settled.

Caesar's army

Apart from Caesar himself, the real hero of the campaign in Gaul was the ordinary Roman legionary. The picture shows him in full battle equipment. He wore a metal helmet with a plume, and hinged cheek-pieces. The body armour was mail (*lorica*), probably attached to a linen corselet, with the shoulder-pieces backed with leather. A leather belt (*cingulum*) was worn round the waist fairly tightly, to take some of the weight of the mail from the shoulders. A sword (*gladius*) and sheath (*vagina*) were carried on the right side. A dagger (*pugio*) was worn on the left side. The shield (*scutum*) was made of layers of leather, rimmed with bronze. The javelin (*pilum* – two were carried into battle) had a shaft of wood, and a pointed section of iron, with a specially softened neck so that it bent on hitting and could not be used by the enemy. Studded leather boots (*caligae*) were worn on the long marches and into battle.

All legionaries were Roman citizens. They enlisted, usually at eighteen, and after satisfying medical inspection were sent to legionary headquarters, where they swore oaths of loyalty to the 'Senate and People of Rome' and often to their commanding officer. Then they went to training camp, where they were taught to use their weapons, dig ditches and ramparts, build camps and march long distances in full equipment. They also learnt a skilled trade, so that the legion provided its own surveyors, stone-masons and engineers, for example.

Eight legionaries formed a *contubernium*, which shared a tent and arrangements for cooking and eating.

This is an enlarged drawing of the gladius worn by the Roman legionary opposite. it is a reconstruction of remains found in the River Thames.

This modern artist's drawing of a Roman legionary soldier of Caesar's time is based on archaeological finds.

This is a modern artist's reconstruction of a Roman army tent. It held 8–10 men and was made from sections of leather sewn together.

Ten *contubernia* formed a *century* (*centuria*), commanded by a centurion (with an *optio* as second in command) – 80 men.

Six centuries formed a *cohort* – 480 men (though the first cohort was nearly twice as large, for all extra non-fighting men, like secretaries, doctors, cooks, and servants, and about 30 horsemen were attached to it).

Ten cohorts formed a *legion* – about 5,000 men.

At its largest Caesar's legionary army numbered under 50,000 men.

Caesar also used thousands of cavalrymen recruited from his Gallic allies, or hired as mercenaries from Spain or Germany. There were also light-armed auxiliary troops in the army, like archers from Crete, or skilled slingers who came from the Balearic Isles; but these non-Roman troops were commanded by Roman officers.

5 The Civil War, 50–45 BC

The end of the triumvirate

Pompey and Crassus as consuls in 55 BC had apparently guaranteed long life for the triumvirate. But in 54 BC, the main link between Caesar and Pompey was broken when Julia died in childbirth. Next, in 53 BC both Crassus and his son Publius were killed in a disastrous war which Crassus had launched against the Parthians in his ambition for military glory. Three legions were wiped out and their standards captured, a disgrace which haunted Rome for years. Caesar offered to divorce his wife Calpurnia and marry Pompey's daughter, while Pompey was to marry Caesar's great-niece Octavia. But Pompey refused, and instead chose the daughter of one of Caesar's enemies. He also preferred to stay in Rome rather than set out for Spain, which his officers governed for him. The triumvirate was dead, and the alliance between Caesar and Pompey was dying.

Warfare between the gangs of Clodius (pro-Caesar) and Milo (pro-Pompey) raged so fiercely in Rome throughout 53 BC that the elections could not be held. In January 52 BC Clodius was killed by Milo's gang. His supporters, in order to make a funeral pyre to burn the body, tore up the wooden benches of the Senate House, which itself then burned down. By a bill of the senate, which Bibulus proposed and Cato supported, Pompey was made 'sole consul' to restore order. With his usual efficiency, Pompey passed new laws against violence and riot, and enforced them with some of the troops from his Spanish command, whom he had kept in Italy. In August this command was prolonged for another five years; Caesar's was not.

Caesar under threat

As he saw Pompey moving closer to the optimates, Caesar had taken steps to protect himself. To make sure that he could move straight from his position as provincial commander in Gaul to a consulship, and so avoid prosecution (see pp. 31–32), all ten tribunes sponsored a bill in the senate allowing him to stand for the consulship *in absentia*, away from Rome. Nor was Pompey yet ready for a complete break. A bill defining the rights of magistrates contained a clause that all candidates for the consular elections must appear in Rome in person. To avoid misunderstanding, Pompey personally added a clause exempting Caesar.

By the summer of 51 BC it was clear that Caesar would soon have won complete victory in Gaul. The optimates were determined that Caesar should be made to hand over his province and his army to a successor so that, before he could stand for election in July 49 BC, he would hold no office and could be prosecuted. The agreement made by the triumvirs in 55 BC (see page 32) that no one should be allowed to propose a successor was forgotten. In 51 and 50 BC a number of such proposals, and other laws aimed at replacing Caesar, were put forward. They were vetoed by tribunes on his behalf. When it was reported that the Parthians were threatening Syria, the senate voted that Pompey and Caesar should each send a legion. Pompey contributed a legion which he had lent Caesar in 53 BC, so that Caesar in effect lost two. When better news arrived from the east, the two legions were kept in Italy. Yet when the optimates constantly implored Pompey to join them openly against Caesar, he wavered, and did nothing.

Caesar versus Pompey

Most people were desperate to avoid civil war. They could see that Caesar would never surrender his position of power, put himself at the mercy of the optimates, or acknowledge Pompey as his superior. A formal motion in the senate, in December 50 BC, that both Caesar and Pompey should give up their commands and disarm, was carried by a vote of 370 to 22. Everyone wanted peace except these 22 extreme optimates. On the next day one of them, the consul Marcellus, ignored the good sense of the majority: when a rumour reached Rome that Caesar's army was crossing the Alps, he rushed from the senate, dramatically thrust a sword into Pompey's hand and begged him to take command of all the forces in Italy, 'to save the republic'. At last Pompey made up his mind, and accepted the challenge.

Caesar is declared a public enemy

Caesar, who was spending the winter in Cisalpine Gaul, tried to reach a compromise. On 1 January 49 BC, a letter from Caesar was read out in the senate offering to give up his command and disarm if Pompey would do the same. The consuls, at Pompey's insistence, would not allow a vote. A motion that Caesar should be declared a public enemy unless he laid down his arms by a certain date, was carried, but vetoed by Marcus Antonius (Mark Antony), one of the new tribunes. Negotiations continued in Pompey's country house. Another offer from Caesar, to keep only one legion and the province of Illyricum, might have been accepted, but for angry opposition again from M. Porcius Cato.

Marcus Antonius c. 83–30 BC. This denarius, issued by Mark Anthony when he was a triumvir, a few years after Caesar's death, gives some idea of his strong-willed character.

Then the senate met again on the 7th, and a decree was passed instructing the consuls to 'see to it that the state came to no harm', a time-honoured formula equivalent to declaring Caesar a public enemy. Two tribunes, Mark Antony and Gaius Cassius, vetoed it. When their veto was disregarded by the hysterical senate, they chose to regard this as a threat to

their lives, and fled to Caesar 'for protection'. The senate proceeded to appoint new governors for all Caesar's provinces, Transalpine Gaul, Cisalpine Gaul and Illyricum.

Throughout the troubled years ahead, Caesar wrote another set of Commentaries, called 'On The Civil War', which were published after his death and have survived to the present day. He describes how, while waiting for news in his province, he told his troops what had been happening in Rome. He records his closing words: 'Under my leadership you have in nine years served Rome with great success; you have won countless battles, and pacified Gaul and Germany: now I am asking you to defend my reputation and position from the attacks of my enemies.'

His account continues: 'The men of the Thirteenth (I had sent for this legion at the start of the troubles, the rest had not yet arrived) clamoured that they were ready to avenge the wrongs done to their general, and to the tribunes of the people.' Caesar had the backing he needed.

Crossing the Rubicon

Caesar at once marched south. By taking an army over the river Rubicon into Italy he was committing treason, and as good as declaring war. The odds were against him. He controlled Gaul and Cisalpine Gaul, but had ony one legion with him, and little support among the politicians in Rome. Pompey, backed by the senate, controlled the rest of Italy and the empire, and was raising troops all over Italy. At the moment, however, Pompey had only two legions, the two which he had taken from Caesar. With his usual speed Caesar swept down the east coast of Italy, and was joined on the way by a number of the soldiers raised by Pompey. At this the consuls and senate left Rome for Capua, while Pompey hurried to raise fresh troops in Apulia.

Then Lucius Domitius Ahenobarbus, just appointed the new governor of Transalpine Gaul, with three newly enrolled legions, was foolish enough to confront Caesar at Corfinium. After a short siege his soldiers surrendered to Caesar, and handed over their commander as well. Ahenobarbus and five other senators caught in the town were set free to join Pompey if they wished. By now two more legions and several thousand Gallic troops had joined Caesar from Gaul. Pompey was outnumbered and had no alternative but to leave Italy for

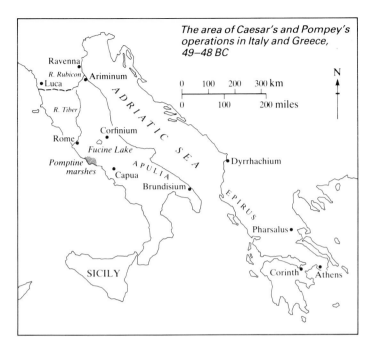

The area of Caesar's and Pompey's operations in Italy and Greece, 49–48 BC

Greece, where he could enrol new legions and summon others from the eastern provinces. On 17 March, taking all the available ships, Pompey sailed from Brundisium. Caesar, who had spent nine days outside the city walls in the hope that diplomacy might yet win Pompey over, was left to watch the ships disappear over the horizon. Though he had failed to catch Pompey, Caesar cannot have been entirely displeased. It was a great psychological advantage to have forced Pompey and his followers to abandon Italy.

During this period Caesar had made three attempts to make peace with Pompey, and when he reached Rome from Brundisium Caesar tried to persuade the few senators who had remained there to reopen peace negotiations. All these attempts failed. Short of cash, Caesar broke into the treasury vaults in the temple of Saturn, which the consuls had forgotten to empty. Then, leaving Marcus Aemilius Lepidus in charge of Rome and Mark Antony in charge of Italy, Caesar hurried to face Pompey's supporters in Spain: he could not afford to leave an enemy army behind him in Spain when he had finally collected enough ships to take his troops against Pompey in Greece. For the moment Pompey himself, still trying to collect an army, could safely be left.

The widespread war

The chart and the map on page 40 show Caesar's movements over the next five years. Every day in Rome was spent in continual political activity aimed at securing his own position and in improving the lot of his fellow citizens. Every day abroad was spent in fighting one campaign against his enemies, and planning the next. Moreover, in his journeys Caesar visited every Roman province, and gained a far broader view of the empire than any other Roman statesman of his age.

Caesar in Spain, 49 BC

Caesar left Rome on 3 April 49 BC. By the 19th he was organising the siege of Massilia in Gaul. After three weeks, leaving some of his army to continue the siege, he marched into Spain, and joined the legions which he had sent ahead. Forty days later, at Ilerda, he had forced the Pompeian army to surrender without a battle by diverting its water supply.

From the siege of Corfinium onward, Caesar was always conscious that he was fighting his fellow citizens. He did everything to avoid bloodshed, always treated his enemies mercifully and set his captives free, even when he knew that they would at once rejoin the struggle against him. This made Caesar popular, and people everywhere began to think that he did have a chance of ultimate victory.

By November Massilia had surrendered. It had been a famous Greek colony. Caesar allowed it to keep its self-government, but took away its territory, on which its power depended, and it soon declined into insignificance.

On his way back to Rome Caesar heard that he had been granted a specific dictatorship to hold elections. He was dictator for eleven days, long enough, with his amazing energy, to pass new laws to recall some exiles, to relieve the hardship of debtors in the current financial crisis (for the war had brought much business to a standstill), and finally to hold elections. It is no surprise that Caesar and a colleague were elected consuls for 48 BC. But Caesar could now rightly claim that he *was* legally the consul, and not the outlaw which his enemies had made him. Of course the optimates, with the bulk of the senate and the two existing consuls, insisted that the legal government rested with *them,* even if it was no longer in Rome.

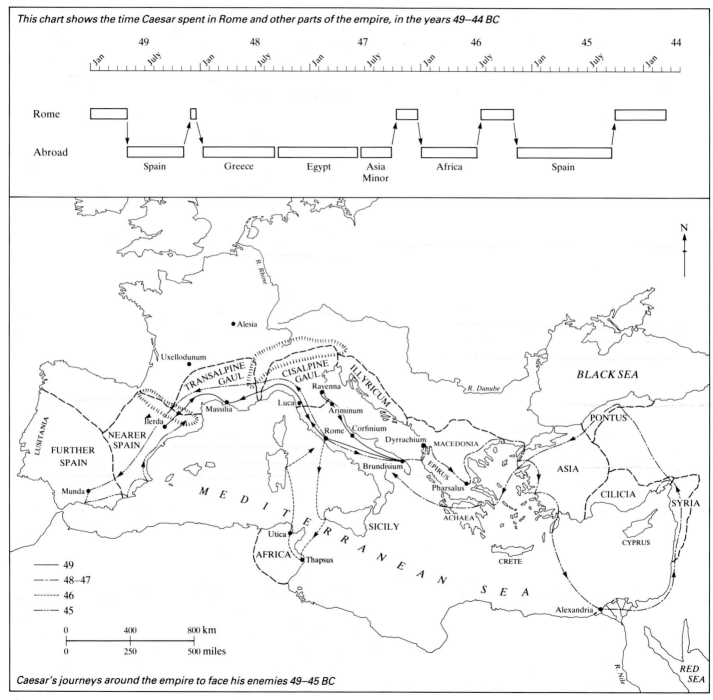

This chart shows the time Caesar spent in Rome and other parts of the empire, in the years 49–44 BC

| | 49 | 48 | 47 | 46 | 45 | 44 |

Rome

Abroad

Spain   Greece   Egypt   Asia Minor   Africa   Spain

— 49
—·— 48–47
‑‑‑ 46
—··— 45

0   400   800 km
0   250   500 miles

Caesar's journeys around the empire to face his enemies 49–45 BC

Caesar faces Pompey in Greece, 48 BC

In Greece Pompey had now mustered 36,000 legionaries, 7,000 cavalry and 300 ships. This fleet, under the command of Bibulus, was massed in the Adriatic to stop Caesar's crossing. Caesar could not afford to let Pompey's forces grow any larger. In early January 48 BC he risked a winter embarkation from Italy, even though he had enough ships for only half his force, some 20,000 men. He landed safely in Epirus, but Bibulus caught thirty transport ships on their way back to pick up the rest of Caesar's troops, killing their captains and crews. Furious that Caesar had escaped him, Bibulus stayed at sea, and it was not till April that Antony could slip through the blockade with four more legions. By this time Bibulus had died of exhaustion.

On land, Pompey and Caesar manoeuvred round each other for weeks along the coast of north-west Greece. When Antony's troops reached him, Caesar tried to blockade Pompey at Dyrrhachium with siege-lines 17 miles (27 km) long. But Pompey easily broke through the lines and defeated his enemy. Caesar's army was now cut off from provisions, so he made for Thessaly and pitched camp in the plain of Pharsalus, where he eventually fought Pompey on 9 August.

The battle of Pharsalus

Pompey's foot-soldiers numbered 47,000 to Caesar's 22,000, his cavalry 7,000 to 800. So confident were the optimates of victory that they spent their time deciding how to divide the offices of state amongst them. Pompey put his faith in a cavalry charge. It swept Caesar's cavalry away, but then met a line of infantry cohorts specially placed to meet them. The infantry did not throw their javelins, but used them to stab: 'Aim at their faces!' Caesar had ordered.

Pompey's cavalry turned tail. And though his infantry easily outnumbered Caesar's, their morale and quality were far inferior. Most of Caesar's men had fought with him all over Gaul, and regarded him with affection as well as awe. Pompey's soldiers were either newly recruited, or had been serving in comfortable eastern provinces without any recent battle experience. Many of them, though fighting 'for liberty', still looked up to Caesar as the people's hero. The battle was long and hard, but when Caesar threw in his reserves, Pompey's

men gave way, and Pompey himself lost his nerve and galloped back to base camp. The battle was over. Of the 15,000 killed, 6,000 were Roman citizens, including Ahenobarbus. Caesar grimly surveyed the scene; '*Hoc voluerunt*' ('They would have it'), he said. Then he offered a complete pardon and freedom to any who would come and ask for it: few did.

Egypt and Asia Minor, 48–47 BC

With a few friends Pompey fled to Egypt, and as he stepped ashore he was murdered, on the order of the boy king Ptolemy's advisers. His head was presented to Caesar, who arrived with a small force three days later. In one way the murder solved a problem, for it would have been difficult for Caesar to offer Pompey the same generosity he had shown lesser opponents, and Pompey would have found it intolerable to be the living example of Caesar's mercy. Yet Caesar was outraged by his death. Pompey had been the greatest Roman of his day, and Caesar's daughter Julia had loved him.

Caesar's contempt for the Egyptians in Alexandria soon aroused their anger and enmity, and they besieged him in the palace during the winter of 48/47 BC, while he awaited reinforcements.

Caesar spent much of his time with Cleopatra, Ptolemy's sister and rival, who put her claims to the throne before the powerful Roman. She smuggled herself into the palace, wrapped in a rolled-up carpet. She was 21, attractive and cultured: she charmed Caesar and became his mistress. When Caesar's reinforcements arrived, Ptolemy's forces were defeated and the young king was killed. Cleopatra was made queen.

Caesar then had to hurry to Asia Minor, where Mithridates' son Pharnaces had invaded the Roman province of Pontus. He defeated Pharnaces in a brilliant five-day campaign, and sent news of his victory to Rome in the famous words, '*Veni, vidi, vici* – I came, I saw, I conquered.'

Caesar returned to Rome in October 47 BC. The next task was to destroy the Pompeians in Africa, whose army had been reinforced by refugees from the battle of Pharsalus. But he had a busy two months in Rome first. Caesar had, in his absence, been declared dictator for a year, with Antony as his *magister equitum* (Master of the Horse and second-in-command), in charge of Rome. Antony had proved a poor administrator. When the dictatorship ended in October,

Caesar dropped Antony and rewarded two others with the consulship for the remaining three months. He himself took the consulship of 46 BC with Aemilius Lepidus.

Meanwhile the veteran soldiers, waiting in Campania to be shipped to Africa, mutinied. They demanded their discharge and the promised rewards. Caesar granted them their demands, and by addressing them as 'Gentlemen', that is as *civilians*, he so shamed them that they now clamoured to be taken to Africa! He sailed for Tunisia with them at the end of November.

Africa, 46 BC

Taking the same risks as in 48 BC Caesar transported his troops through the winter storms in two detachments. His luck held again. After a difficult campaign he routed the Pompeian forces in April 46 BC at Thapsus. In the moment of victory Caesar was unable to control his men, who slaughtered over 10,000 of the enemy. Those who threw themselves on Caesar's mercy were spared; but Cato, in command at Utica, saw that his position was hopeless and committed suicide.

Triumph in Rome

The death of Cato symbolised the death of the republic. When news of the victory reached Rome the senators outdid each other in flattery and devotion – they awarded Caesar four triumphs, for Gaul, Egypt, Pontus and Africa, and thanksgivings to last 40 days. He was made dictator for ten years, and *praefectus morum* (superintendent of morals) for three. Since this office gave him absolute control of the membership of the senate, the senators were putting their careers in his hands. In future magistrates were to be chosen by Caesar, not elected, and in the senate he was to sit between the consuls, with the right to speak first in every debate.

Soon after Caesar reached Rome there were ten days of celebrations: four magnificent triumphs were held over four consecutive days. Shows followed; a wooden amphitheatre with silken awnings was erected; gladiatorial games in memory of Julia were given, in which criminals and condemned captives fought each other on elephants. The first giraffe to be seen in Rome was displayed in a wild beast show. The soldiers were rewarded: legionaries received 5,000 denarii, centurions 10,000 and officers 20,000, and every citizen family had 100 denarii with special gifts of corn and oil.

Caesar granted Cleopatra the title of 'Friend of the Roman People'. Her statue was set up in the temple of Venus, while she herself was installed in Caesar's house on the Janiculum hill with her young son Caesarion, of whom Caesar was almost certainly the father. This move was not very popular, but Caesar's pardon of his enemies was. Cicero publicly praised his generosity, and went on to advise a programme of social reform and reconstruction (see the next chapter). But one campaign still had to be fought.

The last campaign: Spain 46–45 BC

In Spain Pompey's sons had collected thirteen legions. They had been joined by Labienus (he had been Caesar's second-in-command in Gaul, but fought against him in this war) with the veteran remnants from Africa and all those whose hatred of Caesar would not let them accept a pardon. At the beginning of December 46 BC Caesar arrived in the province for his last campaign. Three months of vicious fighting culminated in a bitter battle at Munda; the Pompeians fought so desperately that Caesar's men wavered. Only when he jumped from his horse, seized a shield and forced his way into the front line did things turn his way. For once he made no attempt to restrain his men: 30,000 Pompeian bodies littered the field. Of the officers only Pompey's younger son Sextus escaped.

After Caesar's death, Sextus Pompeius gathered a large fleet and took Sicily. This denarius, which he issued in 44 BC, shows one of his ships and how much he looked like his father. He was eventually defeated by Augustus and killed.

6 Towards the New Rome

Reform and reconstruction

The battle of Munda was won on 17th March 45 BC, but Caesar did not return to Rome until October. He spent seven weeks in Spain founding fifteen new colonies. On his way home he picked sites for two more in Transalpine Gaul, and later ordered others in Greece and Africa. As a result, 20,000 discharged veterans and 80,000 poor citizens from Rome found new homes overseas. In this way he began to give shape to his ideas about the wider empire, in which Roman citizens in all the provinces should have a share, and Rome should not be the only important city. With this aim Caesar granted Roman citizenship to many individuals and communities in the provinces. He introduced a method of paying taxes direct, so that publicani became unnecessary, and he imposed strict controls on the governors of provinces. Most important, he brought some Gallic nobles into the Senate, as a start to wider representation.

Back in Rome, Caesar at once promoted a great number of new laws. He held a census, and reduced the number of people eligible for free corn from 320,000 to 150,000: large families had preference. Murderers were to have all their property confiscated, other major criminals were to lose at least half. (At this time the death penalty was almost always replaced by exile, and wealthy criminals had not suffered much.) Caesar issued a new gold coinage, and planned a public library system, to hold every item of Greek and Latin literature. He reformed the calendar, which was over two months out of step with the natural seasons; this Julian Calendar is still in use, with some slight adjustments by Pope Gregory XIII in AD 1582, which were adopted by Britain in AD 1752.

This modern drawing shows the temple of Venus Genetrix, which dominated the Forum Julium, as it looked in ancient times.

A modern reconstruction drawing of the Basilica Julia, which became the most important law-court in Rome. It was next to the Via Sacra in the Roman forum, and was completed after Caesar's death (the two columns in front were erected much later).

Many of these projects were carried out in Caesar's lifetime or soon after; only Caesar's death stopped the others. The number and variety of them show his ability to reach a decision with amazing speed, and his inexhaustible energy. Rome was intensely busy as drafters of laws, planners, engineers, architects, builders, secretaries and scribes all set feverishly to work. Officials, too, of all grades were needed; accordingly Caesar raised the number of praetors from 8 to 16, the aediles from 4 to 6 and the quaestors from 20 to 40. He also needed to replenish the senate, depleted by the civil war, and its membership was increased to 900. In this way, too, Caesar was able to reward all those who had supported him during the wars.

Building on open spaces in the city was forbidden, except in special circumstances; traffic was restricted (all carts were banned during the daytime except builders' wagons), and the upkeep of the roads was ensured. The Forum Julium was completed. In its centre was a magnificent temple to Venus Genetrix, claimed to be the foundress of the Julian family. Work started in the original Forum on a new basilica (a large hall for public business and justice), which was finished soon after Caesar's death. The Senate House, burnt down by Clodius' thugs, was re-built.

In Italy, money to help Italian industry came from new harbour-dues. To relieve unemployment, at least a third of all herdsmen on the great ranches had to be free men. The membership of local town councils was opened to freedmen (ex-slaves), but barred to gladiators or bankrupts. Architects drew up plans for great projects – a new harbour at Ostia (actually built by the emperors Claudius and Trajan); the draining of the Fucine Lake and Pomptine marshes (achieved respectively by Claudius, and in our own century by Mussolini) to extend agricultural land; a new road across the Apennines. A canal was to be dug across the Corinthian isthmus (often attempted, but never completed until AD 1893).

Honours for Caesar

A few of the new senators were freedmen, centurions or provincials. Over 400 were businessmen and landowners, from all over Italy, and their entry did much to unite the whole country and reduce the unfair dominance of Rome. Despite a small surviving optimate opposition, the new senate owed allegiance to Caesar and was willing to carry out his policies. It went further and voted Caesar a host of honours. He was awarded the titles *Pater Patriae* (Father of his Country) and *Liberator: Imperator* was to be part of his name. His statue was to be placed in all the temples of Rome and the towns of Italy. He was allowed on all occasions to wear a purple triumphal toga, and a laurel wreath, and to use a gilded chair. A temple was to be built to the Mercy of Caesar and an ivory statue of the dictator was to be carried in processions with those of all the gods. (Soon after his death a cult of *Divus Julius* (the god Julius) was established). His birthday was to be a public holiday. We remember best that the month Quinctilis was renamed July in his honour.

Caesar as king?

So many honours were heaped upon Caesar that the plebs became resentful and cynical: he himself tried to reject some which he felt went too far. But he was not unaffected by all this flattery. On one occasion he did not bother to rise from his chair when a deputation of senators came to see him, and this made him intensely unpopular.

Worse was to come. One day in January 44 BC one of Caesar's statues was found wearing a diadem, a headband that was the symbol of oriental kings. Two tribunes had it removed. A few days later he was hailed as *Rex* (King) by a spectator as he rode by. Though he replied that his name was not 'King' but 'Caesar', the same two tribunes had the man arrested. Caesar so disapproved of their attitude that he had the tribunes removed, and their names struck from the roll of senators. Though he did have them reinstated later, the man who had invaded Italy in 49 BC ostensibly to protect the rights of the tribunes was now treating them with a harshness which the optimates had never dared show.

On 15 February Caesar assumed the title *Dictator perpetuus*. He sat on his gilded chair, wearing a purple toga and a golden wreath, watching a festival from a platform in the Forum. As the priests passed by, their leader, the consul Mark Antony, approached Caesar and placed a golden crown on his head. Caesar took it off, to the applause of the crowd. Twice more he rejected Antony's offer, and saying 'Only Jupiter Best and Greatest is king of the Romans' ordered him to take it to Jupiter's temple. We do not know how to interpret this incident. Some people believe that Caesar wanted to be king, and was testing the feelings of the people. If they had cheered when Antony offered the crown, he would have accepted it. Others think that this was a move by his political enemies to embarrass him, and that Antony was misled into accepting the suggestion.

Supreme power

Whatever the truth, one thing was clear: Caesar was now far above other men. From 59 to 49 BC his political actions were constantly affected by his respect for the law that ten years must pass between successive consulships. The change in his regard for the law after that time is clear from the table of Caesar's offices.

It is difficult to find reliable evidence for Caesar's feelings. In a letter to an opponent in 48 BC, he had declared that all he wanted was 'tranquility for Italy, peace for the provinces, security for the empire' – significantly he does not mention Rome. Even in 46 BC, in accepting the honours awarded him after his return from Africa, Caesar had pledged himself to a policy of reconciliation. He had sworn that even the idea of

Caesar's offices, 49–44

49	Dictator for 11 days to hold elections
48 Consul	Dictator for one year, from October
47 (No consuls until Caesar appointed two in October)	Still dictator, till September
46 Consul	In April, Dictator for 10 years
45 Consul by himself; resigned in October, appointing two of his officers in his place	Still dictator
44 Consul, with Mark Antony	In February, dictator for life.

(Caesar had not been given the right to appoint himself or anyone else to the consulship or dictatorship: the assembly of the people simply did what they were told.)

despotism, absolute power, was repugnant to him, and repeated that he had only fought the civil war to save himself from dishonour. Yet he had ridden ruthlessly over all attempts to oppose him. As early as January 49 BC, after asking the remnants of the senate to join him in taking over the government of Rome, he had threatened, 'If you are too timid for the task, I shall not trouble you; I shall govern the state by myself.' Perhaps this reveals his true feelings.

The future of the republic

After his final victory Caesar was constantly receiving advice from Cicero and others about what he must do 'to restore the republic'. But Suetonius quotes him as saying that 'The republic is nothing, a mere name without form or substance.' In truth, Caesar had realised – he was probably the first to do so – that the republic was finished. The careers of men like Marius, Sulla, Pompey and Caesar himself had taught the lesson of how to seize control of the republic, and it was a lesson that any ambitious general could learn. Caesar had skilfully used constitutional elements, the people's assemblies and the tribunate, to thwart the senate. The senate had been dominated by a clique devoted, not to the good of the state as a whole, but to its own advantage. It might be possible to change the senate, transform the tribunate, control the assemblies: but if all that were done, what would be left of the old republic?

If Caesar had any plans for what should replace the republic we do not know what they were. He was master of the Roman world: he did not intend to let it fall into chaos and anarchy. He was now holding permanently the dictatorship, an office intended originally only to tide the republic over a short crisis. With its superiority over all other offices, and freedom from the tribunes' veto, the dictatorship suited Caesar perfectly. For the moment he saw no need to find some other title or position. Clearly some sort of permanent absolute control was required for the future: its exact form was a problem. Caesar intended to set out on 18 March on a campaign against the Parthians which would last three years. Perhaps in that period he would have found the solution.

In the books he wrote himself on the Civil War, and in accounts by other historians, Caesar's dislike of the dishonesty of politicians is apparent. He much preferred the blunt and genuine character of soldiers. He liked being a commander when he could give orders which would be obeyed without question. In Rome he had to persuade, to be careful with his words in case he hurt the tender feelings of some suspicious senator. He found this increasingly distasteful, and often showed his impatience. It is significant that he had spent eleven of the past twelve years with his troops, and as soon as he had returned from Spain he had started planning the invasion of Parthia, to avenge the disgraceful defeat of Crassus.

Conspiracy

Many nobles were offended by Caesar's obvious contempt for political life in Rome. They could not accept that their traditional powers in the senate had been eclipsed, and they bitterly resented his superiority. Throughout his life Caesar had aroused deep feelings. He was either loved or hated; there was no middle course. But now even some of his supporters felt that he had gone too far. The assumption of the perpetual dictatorship was the last straw. A conspiracy of some 60 leading men was formed, led by C. Cassius Longinus. He chose as the figurehead Marcus Junius Brutus, a descendant of the Brutus who had expelled the last king of Rome in 510 BC. Their watchword was 'Freedom'. Since many of the conspirators were men who had supported Caesar, and could therefore expect to be rewarded by him, we must assume that they were sincerely determined to put right an intolerable wrong. They ignored a remark of Caesar's, which proved only too true, that to remove him would only involve the republic in more trouble and civil war.

They knew they must strike before Caesar left to join the army on 18 March. On the morning of 15 March Julius Caesar prepared to attend a meeting of the senate he had summoned. His wife Calpurnia told him of a bad dream which she believed foretold danger for him, and almost dissuaded him from leaving home. But Decimus Junius Brutus, one of the conspirators whom Caesar trusted absolutely, protested that he could hardly send a message to the senate telling them to go away and come back when Calpurnia had better dreams.

As Caesar went through the busy streets, a number of people handed him documents, which he passed to an attendant, to read later. Artemidorus, a Greek philosopher, cried, 'Read this one, Caesar, quickly and by yourself: it's important

The obverse shows Marcus Junius Brutus 85–42 BC, the head of the conspiracy.

The reverse shows the Cap of Liberty, and daggers: the letters EID MAR are abbreviations for an old-fashioned spelling of the Ides of March.

and concerns you personally.' Caesar took it, and was several times on the point of reading it, but was prevented by the people who thronged round him. He was still holding it when he entered the Assembly Rooms and was killed.

After Caesar

As the republic was failing, Caesar's remedy was to win absolute power for himself. He apparently had no long-term solution to the state's problems. His contemporaries, indeed, regarded them as insoluble. After his death one of his friends remarked, 'If Caesar, with all his genius, could not find an answer, who will find one now?' He had acquired almost monarchical power. Though in his will he had left three-quarters of his possessions to his great-nephew Octavius, and had indeed adopted him as his son, he cannot have regarded him as a successor, for he was only eighteen. Mark Antony, who soon took control of Rome, when Brutus and Cassius were forced by the anger and hatred of the people to leave the city, certainly believed that Gaius Julius Caesar Octavianus (Octavius' full name after the adoption) was insignificant.

Within a year, relying on the magic of that name, Octavius had raised an army of Caesar's veterans and won over the affection of the people. He gradually overcame all opposition, until in 30 BC Antony and Cleopatra, after being defeated in a great sea-battle off the coast of Greece, both committed suicide. Octavius was now left unchallenged as master of the Roman world.

Where Julius Caesar failed, Octavius succeeded. He found a way to cloak the autocracy of an emperor in the semblance of republicanism. He ruled for another 45 years, and founded a system of empire which survived for nearly 500 years in Italy, and until AD 1453 in Constantinople. He was soon given the almost mystic name of Augustus, by which we know him. But the title by which he and all his successors were usually called was Caesar; in this way the name of one of the world's greatest generals and politicians was preserved. And in the forms 'Kaiser', 'Tsar' and 'Shah' it has survived to modern times.

Augustus, dressed as an imperator, a statue made shortly after his death; the scene on his breastplate shows the recovery of the standards lost to the Parthians by Crassus, which Augustus achieved by diplomacy, not war.

Glossary

aedile one of 4 officials, 2 patrician (called curule aediles) and 2 plebeian, who were in charge of water supply, street-cleaning, traffic, building regulations, etc. in the city.

censor one of 2 officials whose duty was to check the list of senate members and remove any whose conduct had shown them to be unsuitable, make public works contracts and sell the right to collect taxes.

centuria a company of soldiers, in practice about 80 strong, made up of 10 contubernia.

cognomen the third name of a patrician, indicating the branch of the family to which he belonged, e.g. Cicero.

cohort a unit of troops consisting of 6 centuriae (centuries).

consul one of the 2 chief officials in the Roman republic; chosen from the senate, they were elected by the people to serve for one year.

contubernium a group of about 8 soldiers sharing a tent and feeding arrangements.

cursus honorum the formal 'career structure' for public service: magistracies were held in a strict order.

dictator an official appointed in times of crisis; he had power over all other magistrates and supreme military command.

fasces bundles of rods that were carried before the highest magistrates, each bundle containing an axe as a symbol of authority to punish. The number of fasces was an indication of the magistrate's rank.

gladius a fairly short sword, mainly for thrusting, worn at a soldier's right side.

Imperator a title originally signifying 'Commander-in-Chief'; it later became the title of the Roman Emperors.

legion the principal unit in the Roman army, made up of 10 cohorts, usually about 5,000 men.

magistrate a government official.

nobiles men of noble (aristocratic) families.

nomen the middle name of a patrician, derived from his *gens*, or 'clan', and usually ending in -ius, e.g. Tullius.

optimates the party of the aristocrats and their supporters. (NB the singular form in Latin is *optimas*, but we generally use the English form instead, and say 'an optimate'.)

patricians members of the Roman nobility; the word comes from *patres*, 'fathers' or 'ancestors'.

plebiscitum a decree passed by the assembly of the plebs.

plebs (plebeians) the non-patrician section of the populus; its assembly could be summoned at any time by the tribunus plebis, and could pass decrees (plebiscita).

pomoerium the city boundary of Rome, outside which a victorious general had to wait while the grant of a triumph was being decided; anyone who wanted to be a candidate in an election had to be inside it.

Pontifex Maximus the High Priest; this was a position of little power, but immense prestige.

populares (singular: popularis) the party of those who did not belong to one of the powerful aristocratic families.

populus the whole body of (male) Roman citizens, including both patricians and plebeians.

praenomen the forename of a patrician; only a man's family or close friends would address him by this name, which in writing was often abbreviated to an initial, e.g. M. Tullius Cicero.

praetor a magistrate concerned with administering justice; after spending a year as a praetor, a man was eligible to become a provincial governor.

province a territory, outside Italy, acquired by the Romans and brought under Roman rule as part of Rome's empire.

publicani private companies who bid for the right to collect the taxes from a particular province.

quaestor one of 20 magistrates, 2 of whom were in charge of the Roman treasury, while the rest were assistants to provincial governors, being particularly concerned with finance.

scutum a large military shield, made of layers of leather stitched together and surrounded with a bronze rim.

senate the council which was the main governing body of the Roman state; in Caesar's time it had around 600 members.

tribunus militum a subordinate military officer.

tribunus plebis one of 10 officials, chosen from the plebs; one of them acted as president of the people's assembly; all had the right to veto any decree of the senate or the assembly.

triumph a triumph was usually granted to a Roman general after an outstanding victory. A great parade took place, with senators, magistrates and important prisoners participating; captured booty was displayed on wagons.

Triumvirate, the First the pact between Caesar, Pompey and Crassus (60 BC), by which they secured a commanding position in the state.